The Fatherstyle Advantage

The Fatherstyle Advantage

Surefire Techniques Every Parent Can Use to Raise Confident and Caring Kids

Kevin O'Shea & James Windell

STC PAPERBACKS

Stewart, Tabori & Chang
New York

Editor: Jennifer Levesque
Designer: 3+Co.
Production Manager: Kim Tyner

Library of Congress Cataloging-in-Publication Data
O'Shea, Kevin, 1962-
The fatherstyle advantage : surefire techniques every parent can use to raise confident and caring kids / by Kevin O'Shea and James Windell.
p. cm.
Includes bibliographical references and index.
ISBN: 1-58479-477-1
1. Child rearing. 2. Father and child. 3. Parenting. I. Title: Father style advantage.
II. Windell, James. III. Title.
HQ769.O776 2006
649'.1—dc22 2005031328

Published in 2006 by Stewart, Tabori & Chang
An imprint of Harry N. Abrams, Inc.

The text of this book was composed in
Din & Ehrhardt MT

Printed and bound in
the United States of America
10 9 8 7 6 5 4 3 2 1

harry n. abrams, inc.
a subsidiary of La Martinière Groupe

115 West 18th Street
New York, NY 10011
www.hnabooks.com

Dedication

To Mairen, Declan, and Conall, who each remind me of the joys and challenges of parenthood every day
K.O.

To Jane and Jonathan; Jill and Jason
J.W.

CONTENTS

Introduction

"What a father says to his childen is not heard by the world, but is heard by posterity."

—Jean Paul Richter

This book has a simple premise: that we can all become better parents by adopting some of the practices of today's most involved fathers. If you're amused by this unusual idea, then you'll find this book full of new and valuable information. If, on the other hand, you find it hard to believe that men have something special to offer when it comes to parenting, then this book is one you definitely must read. But even if you already know that fathers bring unique gifts to parenting, this book will show you how you can put some of these gifts to work to become a dramatically better mother or father.

We have recently embarked on a new century in which parenting has become an increasingly shared undertaking. Despite more demands in the workplace, American fathers today are spending substantially more time caring for their children than they were twenty-five years ago. Indeed, fathers spend almost five hours more time in direct parenting activities each week, or roughly 250 more hours in a year, than they did in 1980. That amounts to over six weeks of eight-hour days every year, an astounding social change in such a short time.

But it's not just a matter of more time spent with their children. Fathers have a powerful contribution to make to the raising of children, one that has the potential to help all mothers and fathers become happier, more effective parents. That's why we wrote this book. In this book you will learn about *fatherstyle,* our name for the things that effective fathers do to raise confident and caring children. The five elements of fatherstyle are:

1. *Playactivity*
2. *Promoting Independence*
3. *Nurturing Empathy and Emotional Intelligence*
4. *Solving Discipline Problems while Teaching Children Self-Control*
5. *Creating a Culture of Expectation in the Home*

In the main chapters of this book, we describe how fathers make their invaluable contribution in each of these areas. Of course, we both believe that the best way to raise a child today is to have two active, highly involved parents working closely together in a loving, cooperative team. *Both* mother and father make an important and essential contribution to parenting. Having said that, however, we want to balance the playing field a bit for fathers. The fact is that for most of recent history fathers have been excluded and forgotten as parents, confined to a narrow role as breadwinner. While fathers were permitted to act as occasional playmates and, for older children, disciplinarians, the "real" work of parenting was done by mothers.

But fathers always have always played a major role in child rearing. In the 1950s and 1960s psychological and sociological researchers finally began to recognize this reality by including dads in their studies of parenting. And what did they find? That fathers were playing an amazing, unsung role in the healthy socialization of their children. The research discovered that in some areas, dads were the most important parent.

Recent books such as Kyle Pruett's *Fatherneed: Why Father Care Is as Essential as Mother Care for Your Child* and Ross Parke and Armin Brott's

Throwaway Dads: The Myths and Barriers That Keep Men from Being the Fathers They Want to Be have pointed out the essential role fathers play in raising of their children. We are taking this concept a giant step further, explaining what effective dads do best and letting you know how you—whether you are a mother or father—can adapt their methods to improve your parenting.

You may be wondering about who we are and how we came to write this book. Kevin O'Shea is a Harvard Law School graduate who left his successful legal career to become a full-time father when his first child was born more than eight years ago. Kevin and his wife, Molly, a busy pediatrician, now have three active children, and Kevin is more involved than ever. His many encounters with other active fathers led him to form Partnership for Dads, a nonprofit organization that works with existing institutions to help fathers become more involved parents. Kevin's group grew so rapidly that in 2005 it was selected as the Michigan affiliate of the National Fatherhood Initiative, the nation's premier fatherhood education and advocacy organization. He now conducts workshops for fathers and mothers, speaks to groups about the importance of fathers' involvement, and writes a monthly column on fatherhood for Michigan's largest parenting magazine.

James Windell is a psychologist, parent trainer, and popular newspaper columnist, as well as the author of several parenting and medical books. He was a more traditional father when his two children were growing up, but he was always a very involved parent. And although Jim was divorced from Jill and Jason's mother when they were young, their amicable co-parenting arrangement meant that parenting was always a shared relationship, even though they shared the task from two different households. His own children are now adults, but Jim is still very involved in raising his teenage stepson.

The two of us first met several years ago when Molly O'Shea invited us to speak to the Michigan chapter of the American Academy of Pediatrics. Our friendship grew when we were both speakers and board members for Dads Empowered, a nonprofit group that promotes active fatherhood. Our work on the annual Michigan Fathers Conference, an event that brings together several hundred fathers for a day of education and inspiration each fall, led directly to this book. Together with our wives, we had dinner with Ross Parke, the author and parenting researcher who was a special guest for the conference. We were impressed by Parke's research into fathering, his enthusiasm for parenting his own children, and the book he co-authored with Armin Brott. That dinner ultimately led Kevin to approach Jim with an idea for a new book of our own.

We started out intending to write a book about full-time fathers. As we explored the idea further, however, we came to realize that we wanted to include all involved fathers. As a result, this is the first parenting book featuring advice based on the experiences of fathers. We firmly believe that everyone can learn from America's most effective dads. Some happen to be, like Kevin, full-time, stay-at-home fathers, but the vast majority have a more traditional career and schedule.

What We Are Not Saying

Offering parenting advice can be a sensitive undertaking. The reactions we have received from friends, colleagues, and editors during the process of developing this book have convinced us to make it clear at the outset what we are *not* saying in this book.

First, the purpose of this book is certainly not to prove that fathers are (or can or should be) better parents than mothers. There are plenty of fantastic moms and dads out there. Many of them need no improvement. By the same token, many very involved fathers do a poor job of parenting. Moreover, this book is not meant as a criticism of fathers who, for whatever reason, are not involved parents. In the real world, we each have very different situations and demands, and we believe firmly that nothing is to be gained by hectoring fathers into spending more time with their children. For many men, that's impossible. For the rest, sending a negative message risks making it less likely that they will listen.

Second, we are not claiming that all involved fathers are fatherstyle parents. Observations based on gender are only generalizations. Just as not all men enjoy sports, not all fathers fit the fatherstyle model. By the same token, some mothers do. When we refer to fathers (and mothers) throughout this book, we are talking about *most* fathers and *most* mothers. Nor is our aim to imply that there is something wrong with fathers and mothers who don't fit the fatherstyle mold. We don't employ every one of the fatherstyle techniques we describe in the pages that follow. Moreover, every parent has a special style that it would be all but impossible for other parents to adopt.

Third, we are not arguing that the unique parenting style of involved fathers is the result of some biological imperative. Many authors have made this claim, but it is a subject we choose not to address. We are neither biologists nor social scientists. For all we know it is entirely possible that fatherstyle parenting is the exclusive result of culture and upbringing. After all, traditional gender roles are still rigorously enforced in our culture, notwithstanding efforts to the contrary. Suffice it to say that most involved fathers employ one or more of the elements of fatherstyle parenting. We will occasionally discuss the reasons, but we will do our best to steer clear of the nature/nurture debate.

Finally, we do not mean to imply that parenting is a competition. Everyone already knows the parenting strengths mothers have. This book demonstrates how involved fathers tend to excel at certain aspects of parenting—an idea that may come as a surprise to a lot of people. It is long past time to acknowledge that mothers do not have a monopoly on good parenting practices. Indeed, the last chapter of the book is devoted entirely to helping couples understand how they can combine their unique *and equally valid* parenting styles to raise happier, healthier children.

What is the Fatherstyle Advantage?

We've already said a few words about fatherstyle, but you may be curious as to what exactly is the *fatherstyle advantage*. It is a two-fold concept. First, it refers to the things that fathers tend to do best when it comes to parenting. Together, the five elements we listed on page 10, which form the heart of this book, create an advantage in parenting skills and style in these distinct areas.

Second, the fatherstyle advantage refers to the extra edge that children get from the way dads raise them differently. This is a boost that makes them more likely to grow into happy, successful adults. The fatherstyle elements are not only great skills for a father; when combined with the good qualities we associate with motherhood, they are bound to benefit children in the best possible ways. We hope to make it plain that fatherstyle parenting can make a positive, lasting difference for mothers, fathers, and most important, their children.

Things to Come

We've laid out this book in a logical progression. We begin with ideas and practices that are most relevant to parents of very young children (such as play, independence, and discipline) and move on to those that have greater meaning for parents of older children (such as emotional intelligence and expectations). Every chapter builds on those that come before, and you will find us repeating early lessons throughout the book in new contexts. That said, every chapter has important information for you regardless of the ages of your children.

Beginning with Chapter 1, we discuss the stereotypes and preconceptions that form our collective view of the proper role of mothers and fathers. We describe some of the research that establishes fathers' unique contributions to effective parenting. We define fatherstyle in greater detail and demonstrate how each of the five elements of fatherstyle can play an important part in a new approach to parenting.

The play style of dads is central to the differences between moms and dads. It is no exaggeration to say that nearly every benefit that comes from fathers' different parenting style radiates from their play. That, indeed, is central to the fatherstyle advantage. Chapter 2 describes how involved fathers use the power of "playactivity" to stimulate children's emotional and intellectual development. We describe how a fathers' playactive style can help his children learn how to get along well with others and to develop better, longer-lasting friendships as they grow. Chapter 2 also describes in detail the playactive techniques you can learn in order to stimulate your young children's development. We even provide specific exercises you can use to master this approach.

We then explain how the concept of playactivity is important not only for infants and toddlers, but is vital to the success of children right through adolescence. As children grow older, fathers' playactive approach translates into an exciting style of child-rearing, challenging children with new situations and providing them with the confidence and skills they need to lead happy, productive lives.

Chapter 3 uses playactivity as a point of departure to reveal how fatherstyle helps children develop independence by taking risks to learn skills and gather information about their world. Not coincidentally, the more children act independently, the more confidence they develop in their ability to handle challenges and adapt to new situations. This increased self-confidence is well-founded. We describe research establishing that children who are permitted to act more independently are more competent and self-confident in all of their endeavors.

This chapter also features advice on how you can encourage your children's independence even in the midst of today's heightened concerns about safety. For example, you will learn more about how and when real-life fathers promote their children's independence and how you can adopt their practices in your own family.

In Chapter 4 we address the key issue that causes parents the most frustration of all: discipline. Parents today are more uncertain than ever about how to handle discipline, something both authors witness firsthand in their regular appearances before parent workshops. Jim notes that every one of the dozens of presentations he makes to parents each year ends up being a discussion of discipline problems and issues. "I recently talked to an audience of fifty parents who came to an evening ostensibly to talk about how to help their children with their homework," Jim recalls. "The main topics of discussion ended up being such things as bedtime struggles, non-compliance with parental requests, meal-time problems, aggressiveness, and finding effective discipline methods." Kevin couldn't agree more: "Unlike most fathers, I get to talk to mothers every day about what concerns them most," he says. "It's discipline. Many mothers I know feel that they are unable to effectively control their children. They are desperate for help."

We deal head-on with parents' confusion over discipline in this chapter. We find that more and more parents are too reluctant to impose rules and do not back them up with meaningful consequences when they are broken. Indeed, it is not too harsh to conclude that many parents are failures when it comes to disciplining their children.

Chapter 4 includes what we think you will find to be one of the most useful features of this book. This is what we call "the magnificent seven": the key techniques that effective fathers use to discipline their children. We describe and discuss each technique in detail, using real-world examples, so that you can begin using them right away to eliminate discipline problems in your home.

The chapter closes with a list of practical steps you can take to "discipline like a dad" by establishing clear expectations, setting well-defined rules, and finding the courage to hold children accountable for their behavior—and misbehavior.

What about so-called emotional intelligence? Perhaps the one area in which everyone would agree mothers have the advantage over fathers is imparting compassion and empathy to their children. Chapter 5, however, debunks this conventional wisdom with long-term research that shows that dads may actually play a bigger role in helping children develop empathy than mothers. More recent studies confirm that fathers are just as empathetic and as capable of nurturing behavior as are mothers. Pioneering psychologist Ross Parke concludes that fathers make an important but often unrecognized contribution to the development of their children's emotional intelligence, what he calls a "contribution that lasts a lifetime."

We explain in Chapter 5 why dads are so good at helping children develop crucial social skills. The surprising findings of studies over the past several years prove that highly involved fathers raise children who are well socialized and who can handle conflict and aggression in more responsible ways than their fatherless peers. We conclude Chapter 5 with some practical strategies you can use to foster emotional intelligence in your own child.

Chapter 6 moves the fatherstyle discussion further, demonstrating how fathers use "expectation parenting" to help their growing children become happy, achievement-oriented adults who demand the best from themselves. The expectation of achievement has been described as an important trait most often related to father care. Kyle Pruett notes that not only do fathers support novelty-seeking behavior in children, but fathers also teach their children to tolerate frustration when attempting something new.

In other words, while mothers typically intervene to "teach" children how to complete a task, fathers prefer to hang back and permit their children to become frustrated before stepping in. The chapter suggests that it is precisely through their willingness to permit their children to experience and overcome frustration that fathers communicate a powerful expectation that their children will succeed. This expectation has been shown to be particularly strong in the case of older children and daughters, who often cite it as a crucial element in their upbringing.

Chapter 6 also shows how the element of expectation that is central to fatherstyle can make children more successful in school, especially in the years when parents typically become less involved in their children's lives. We present dramatic statistics from the largest study ever done on the effect of fathers' involvement at school revealing that fatherstyle can make a substantial, positive contribution to children's education. Most important, we describe the specific things you can do to duplicate that effect.

The chapter ends with more practical recommendations—ways you can develop appropriate expectations for your children and learn to permit them to overcome their natural frustrations so they can succeed and gain the self-confidence they will need in so many areas of their lives.

We devote Chapter 7 to a wide-ranging examination of what separates mothers and fathers and how they can combine their approaches to produce a new, better way to parent. We will re-emphasize that our aim throughout has been to bring some much-needed balance to parenting advice by pointing out that fathers have a lot to teach all parents about good parenting.

Although it is ideal to have both a mother and a father working together, the reality is that many moms and dads are single parents. We want to emphasize that this doesn't mean you can't be an effective parent, nor that you'll be unable to use the fatherstyle approach. We believe that fatherstyle will enhance the parenting skills of any parent—even a single parent going it all alone.

In this final chapter, we introduce the six-part fatherstyle framework, a cooperative approach for integrating different parenting styles. We will explain how couples can use this framework to formulate positions on common parenting problems, such as whining, failure to do chores, back talk, and refusal to participate in family activities. We will show parents how to turn their positions into scripts in advance, how they can use the scripts to respond to varied situations, and how they can revise their approach after evaluating feedback from each other. Finally, we discuss what mothers and fathers can do to resolve conflicts that arise from their different parenting styles.

Special Features of This Book

This book includes a number of features designed to clearly communicate the elements of fatherstyle. These include enlightening and useful dialogues between Jim and Kevin concerning some of the most controversial problems confronting parents today. Also, each chapter includes sidebars with additional materials and discussions that supplement the main text. Most important, we also include the opinions and real-life experiences of many involved fathers, including the candid and surprising insights of a panel of such fathers convened expressly for the purposes of the book.

Our goal is to provide a practical parenting resource that is backed up by the latest research and the experiences of successful parents. It is our hope that the format we have chosen will permit you to get the most out of this book by reading it now and then returning to it again and again as you confront specific parenting challenges.

Before we get to Chapter 1 we would like to point out some stylistic aspects of our writing approach that you may have already noticed. We have written our personal experiences in the third person, rather than using the more awkward "I" and having you trying to guess who is speaking. For example, in Chapter 3, Jim writes about observing fathers and mothers bringing their children to school. (We hasten to point out that Jim doesn't do this very often and he wasn't suspected of being a dangerous stranger!) On the occasions when we each speak in the first person, we use italics for clarity. When we quote from dads or moms, we use only their first names. We want to protect the privacy of parents who have been kind enough to answer our questions, attend our parenting panel, or attend workshops or discussions we've led.

A Final Word

We sincerely hope that the tone of this book reflects the friendship and easy working relationship the two of us have established. It's not always easy to collaborate on a sometimes complicated and intensive project like this one. However, we found ourselves in agreement about most things and the sense that we have a very important message to communicate helped to make for a very smooth working relationship. Since we enjoyed writing this book, we hope it will be just as enjoyable for you to read it. And we hope that it helps to make you a better parent.

Please feel free to contact us with your comments or questions after you've finished the book. Vist our Web site at www.thefatherstyleadvantage.com for a wealth of useful parenting resources, including the opportunity to chat with us about your concerns. After all, we're parents, too, and there's a lot we can learn from one another.

1

Fatherstyle

The New Revolution in Parenting

"Fathers should be neither seen nor heard. That is the only proper basis for family life."

—Oscar Wilde

For much of history it was assumed that a father's role in child rearing was at best tangential, as an assistant to the mother. The above quote from Oscar Wilde, a twist on the well-known maxim about children, reflects this traditional view. A father's role, it was long believed, was to serve as family provider. His role in raising the children was typically limited to disciplinarian and general moral instructor.

But a seismic shift has taken place over the last several decades. The involvement of fathers in day-to-day child rearing has exploded. Today's fathers spend far more time caring for their children than fathers at any point in history. A University of Illinois study found that fathers are spending 66 percent as much time with their children as mothers, up from 50 percent twenty years ago. Moreover, the Changing Workforce survey of 2,877 workers indicates that fathers today are spending thirty minutes more each weekday and one hour more each day on weekends caring for and spending time with their children than they were in 1977. And the number of stay-at-home fathers has more than doubled since 1986, from 1.5 million to almost 3 million in 2005.

This revolution in parenting has dramatically increased our understanding of the importance of involved fathering. The increase in divorced families and the dramatic rise in the numbers of fatherless children have also contributed to a body of scientific literature celebrating the importance of involved fathers in the lives of children. In the early twenty-first century it is no longer a secret that fathers have a vital role to play in the healthy development of their children. There is no longer any question that dads *do* matter.

Vive la Différence

The greater involvement of fathers in child rearing has led to another important development: an understanding that fathers have a fundamentally different approach to parenting than mothers. Enough research has been compiled to establish definitively that *most* fathers parent differently than *most* mothers when they are given the opportunity to be the parent in charge. This finding is not surprising in light of our understanding that most men and most women see the world differently. The work of Deborah Tannen and others has gone a long way to bringing these differences to the attention of a popular audience.

The results of controlled parenting studies have been increasingly supplemented by anecdotal experiences of the millions of families in which fathers are either the primary caregivers or equal partners in child rearing. For the first time in history it is possible for us to compare the practices of involved fathers side-by-side with traditional approaches to parenting.

Today's involved fathers are proving every day that not only can they handle the job, but they also have something unique and powerful to teach their fellow parents about how to contribute to their children's healthy and happy development. This groundbreaking and provocative proposition is what *The Fatherstyle Advantage* is all about. In this book we describe precisely how all mothers and fathers can adopt the techniques and practices that the most involved fathers have developed to become happier, more effective parents. We draw upon the collective wisdom and candid opinions of hundreds of fathers together with the very latest parenting research to provide valuable insights and practical advice to present a new model for parenting called "fatherstyle." We believe that fatherstyle has enormous potential to forever change the way we look at parenting.

Before we talk about the specifics of fatherstyle, however, let's take a brief detour to examine parenting stereotypes and the confusion over the changing roles of mothers and fathers in the early twenty-first century.

Parenting Stereotypes

Society's view of parenthood has long been dominated by stereotypes of the ideal, nurturing mother and her counterpart, the clueless, emotionally distant father. In fact, as a society we associate those qualities normally reserved for motherhood to define what we mean by a good parent. Many people are still confused by the notion that men might be capable of good parenting.

Even our language reflects this bias. For example, the word "maternal" has exclusively positive connotations. Look up "maternal" in a thesaurus and you will find synonyms such as affectionate, kind, devoted, tender, and sympathetic. By contrast, "paternal" has less flattering, and even negative, connotations. Its synonyms include vigilant, overbearing, and possessive. We've all heard of the maternal instinct, a reference to that supposedly natural affinity and skill women have for parenting. Has anyone ever heard of the *paternal* instinct? What would that involve in our mother-centered parenting universe? The natural ability to find a high-paying job and coach Little League?

The popular media supports this idealization of mothers at the expense of fathers. With a few notable exceptions, television and movies have portrayed fathers most often as objects of ridicule. Moreover, the past twenty years have witnessed a rise in what has been called "the new momism," a celebration of mothers as the best primary caretakers for their children. Parenting books and magazines follow this pattern, extolling and encouraging women to reach their full potential as idealized mothers while treating fathers as little more than large children. Kevin was at a school district function where he was one of only a few fathers among about fifty women. As the participants introduced themselves, one woman said she had no children, only a husband. "Same thing," the moderator (a woman) quipped, causing a roar of knowing laughter.

The stereotype of the all-competent mother and the hapless father is so prevalent that even those who condemn it acknowledge its power. In their polemic *The Mommy Myth,* Susan J. Douglas and Meredith W. Michaels argue that our culture's idealized view of mothers actually harms women by sending the message that "if they don't have a small drooling creature who likes to stick forks in electrical outlets, they are leading bankrupt, empty lives." Nevertheless, Douglas and Michaels themselves merrily engage in the father-bashing that is an everyday part of our culture:

> *[M]any of us, having left a child home in the care of a man to return to find the kid eating Slim Jims and marshmallows for dinner and the floor covered with spilled Coke, dirty socks, and guinea pig excrement, have concluded that men can't do it, so we shut them out and do it ourselves. We resent men for not helping us more, but also bask in the smugness that at least here, in this one role, we can claim superiority.*

And this is from two researchers who believe that the idealization of mothers is a *bad* thing!

The reemergence of so-called family values in the political arena has also reinforced the traditional notion that fathers have no business raising their own children. David Blankenthorn of the Institute for American Values has scorned involved fathers for "helping out in order to share equally in the work, joys, and responsibilities of domestic life." These men, he says, have denied their own masculinity. "The New Father model is a mirage," he declares. "There is no father there."

Even feminist leaders, who originally embraced the notion of equally shared parenting, soon reversed direction and embraced the party line that men are simply incapable of parenting as well as women. Letty Cotton Pogrebin, co-founder of *Ms.* magazine, declared in 1990 that fathers are "pathological bullies who abuse their children." Barbara Jordan, the eloquent former congresswoman from Texas and a hero of the Democratic Party, announced that "women have a capacity for understanding and a compassion which a man structurally does not have, does not have it because he cannot have it. He's just incapable of it." Sadly, these views still reflect mainstream thought.

The parenting literature reinforces our stereotypes about the relative child rearing abilities of mothers and fathers. Several hundred books on motherhood were published between 1970 and 2000, the vast majority after 1980. During the same period only a few dozen books have been published for fathers. Even those tended to be how-to guides, including many that apparently assume men will find it challenging to hold a baby without dropping it on its head. By contrast, the cultural notion of the omnicompetent mother is so prevalent that there is only a handful of books that include such basic advice for mothers. Despite the modern reality that most young women have no more advanced knowledge of parenting than do young men, the fiction that girls are somehow naturally prepared for parenthood continues.

The growth of parenting magazines during the past twenty years mirrors this pattern. *Parents*, *Parenting*, *Child*, and *American Baby* are all openly geared to mothers, featuring headlines such as "Moms Guide to the Best New Toys" and "How Busy Moms Do It." Many of these publications have special sections for mothers in every issue. Needless to say, there are no correspon-ding sections for fathers. *Dads*, the only magazine ever aimed at fathers, lasted exactly two issues.

But these parenting stereotypes, strong as they have proven to be, are no longer the only game in town. Rapid social change in the last half of the twen-tieth century has created flexibility, and confusion, regarding the proper role of mothers and fathers.

The Challenge of Changing Roles

In the postwar era our notions of the proper roles of men and women under-went a radical transformation. The Ozzie and Harriet ideal of the late 1940s and 1950s was forever upended by increasing affluence and Betty Friedan's groundbreaking book *The Feminine Mystique* in 1963. The idea that home and motherhood could be an unfulfilling trap rather than the mark of a happy life was part of a cultural journey that led to the women's liberation movement of the later 1960s and 1970s. Women flooded into the workforce, divorce rates increased steeply, and the demand for equality between the sexes bred confusion over who was supposed to do what.

We are still in the midst of that confusion. While no one challenges the right of women to work (and, increasingly, the right of men to be at-home parents), for many mothers and fathers life on the home front is rife with unresolved issues. Many women remain intensely dissatisfied with their lot, resentful that their life decisions are still fodder for social approbation. In 2004 and 2005 alone, three popular books were published that complained, in the angriest tone imaginable, about what they contend is the lie of happy motherhood. Damned if they are mothers (at-home or otherwise), and damned if they're not, many women feel, they are still getting the short end of social change.

At the same time, men also find themselves adrift in a sea of conflicting social demands. Now that their wives are providers, too, and fathers are criticized if they fail to take a more active role in child rearing, men can no longer simply put in their time at the office and put their feet up at home. Many of these men believe, however, that they will be criticized whether they try to become an active parenting partner or not.

But despite skepticism from many quarters, and complaints about "the second shift" that finds working women in dual-career families handling most of the child care and housework, there is no question that American fathers are spending more time than ever caring for their children. Despite a lack of training and persistent cultural pressure to leave the child care to their wives, today's involved fathers are feeding and diapering their babies, dressing and playing with their toddlers, taking their older children to school and sporting events, and even helping with homework.

The greater involvement of today's fathers is finally being reflected in the mass media. Not only in the 2004 blockbuster film *Finding Nemo,* but other portrayals of family life are increasingly likely to show both parents as being actively engaged in the lives of their children. Rosalind Barnett and Caryl Rivers note that "powerful messages about men's caring qualities are reaching larger and larger audiences." The National Fatherhood Initiative, the country's premier fatherhood education and advocacy group, now gives annual awards to companies that do the best job portraying fathers in a positive light in their advertisements.

Perhaps more significantly, social expectations regarding a father's role have also undergone a dramatic transformation. Surveys reveal that young fathers, not content to bring home a paycheck and leave the child rearing to their wives, now expect to be an active part of their children's lives. But while these young dads are willing and able to take an active part in child rearing, from feeding, diapering, and comforting infants to devoting evenings and weekends to helping with homework and other family activities with older children, they receive little support in the workplace and resistance from wives who may guard their traditional territory with a vengeance.

A Modern Parenting Crisis

Not surprisingly, this volatile cultural stew of changing expectations, demands, and realities has led to a modern parenting crisis. Today's parents are turning to ever more specific and proscriptive sources for help in raising their children. No longer convinced that parenting problems can be solved with a copy of Dr. Spock and advice from Grandma, modern mothers and fathers have fed an industry of advice, therapy, and medication that has reached a level unimaginable to the previous generation. Advice books have become almost comically focused on narrow subjects, from how to get your children to go to sleep to when it's wise to take away the pacifier. The use of behavior-modification medications for children has become so widespread that it has created a backlash industry of books and non-medical therapies.

And still it's not enough. In early 2005 the *New York Times* reported on the booming demand for "parent coaches"—individuals paid to help busy parents deal with problems such as temper tantrums and failure to do homework on time. Magazines promise instant cures for terrible toddlers. Television offers *Supernanny* and *Nanny 911*, popular reality shows in which experts in Mary Poppins garb swoop in and provide parenting makeovers. Compared to the polite charges Julie Andrews dealt with, however, the children featured in these programs are frightening monsters, fully capable of inflicting serious bodily harm. The message? Parents today have no idea what they're doing.

We firmly believe that mothers and fathers are not clueless dolts. Today's parents are no less competent and committed than parents of earlier genera-

The Gatekeeping Mother

Though few people are familiar with the term, the *gatekeeping mother* is a staple of the fatherhood literature. She earns her name by jealously guarding her husband's access to their children, insisting that he limit his role to assistant parent and follow her way of parenting. We're all familiar with the mother who won't let her husband feed the baby ("you're holding him wrong"), dress the toddler ("that doesn't go together"), and even play with the children ("you're too rough"). Over time, the gatekeeping mother (and, often, the gatekeeping mother-in-law), can so undermine a father's confidence that he gives up and settles for being an assistant parent.

Kyle Pruett devotes a whole section of his book *Fatherneed* to gatekeeping mothers:

"Pamela Jordan's research at the University of Washington tells repeatedly of the desire in women to be 'first among equals' when it comes to managing the nurturing domain. Women cling to control to the point of micromanaging, especially when they are working, to reassure themselves and reaffirm their competence and essential goodness as mothers. They often overtly discourage paternal involvement in child and domestic care because of their time-honored belief that men will screw it up. When they do permit access through the gateway, it is done on their terms, thoroughly managing their husband's behavior with the children."

The gatekeeping mother is a common phenomenon. In *Throwaway Dads,* Ross Parke and Armin Brott reported on a national survey of mothers in which respondents agreed that fathers should play an important role in child rearing, just "not quite as important as mom's." Fully two-thirds of the mothers questioned seemed threatened by the idea of their husbands serving as equal parenting partners. Jim and Kevin hear about the phenomenon from fathers all the time.

The gatekeeping theme arises again and again, particularly as men become more involved in the care of their children. In an essay in *Parenting* magazine entitled "My Husband, the Perfect Mom," Ayelet Waldman expressed the dilemma of mothers when confronted by their

tions. They face many unique challenges against the backdrop of rapid social change, but they are fully capable of doing what is necessary to raise happy, healthy children. And fatherstyle can help them do it.

husbands' unexpected parenting skills. She calls her husband "the feminist's fantasy dad," changing diapers, cleaning the house, and playing with the children. But she is determined to successfully nurse their new baby. Why? Because "breastfeeding is the only thing I can do that his father can't." She declares that the "ideal of egalitarian parenting is not the bliss it seems" because when "your husband is the best mom around, what is there left for you to be? Second best." Waldman admits that she wants "the absolute primacy that defines and accompanies the traditional role of mother" and finds herself "envious of my husband's centrality to my children's lives." She's ultimately happy because the kids come to her to be comforted: "There is, I think, something unique about the comfort a mother provides."

What we'll emphasize later is that Waldman is right: mothers are great at offering comfort. It's one of the aspects of maternal parenting that is unique. But why do so many women cling to the discredited notion that they, not fathers, are the natural caregivers? Barnett and Rivers speculate that "for mothers, the idea of being the primary nurturer is akin to a security blanket, something to hang onto in a time of great change. If mothers believe that their nurturing is unique and can't be duplicated by fathers, then they don't have to worry about losing their status as 'mommy' when they go to work." They note that as fathers begin to take over more of the responsibility for child rearing, such "mothers can breathe easily, comfortable in the knowledge that they are still the supreme nurturer and hence the most important figure in their child's life."

Whatever her motivation, the gatekeeping mother is an essential character in this book. Her strong desire to be in charge of the parenting is understandable, but it is no longer desirable or tenable. Mothers themselves must accept the fact that they do not have all the answers, nor are they uniquely suited to serve as primary caregivers of their children. In Chapter 7 we will describe how mothers and fathers can work together to provide their children with the best that *both* their parents have to offer.

Recognizing Fatherstyle

Until recently, of course, it has not been possible to determine precisely how the parenting styles of fathers and mothers differ because few men chose to undertake the traditionally female role of child rearing. That has all changed: the homes of the millions of full-time fathers and actively involved traditional fathers are living parenting laboratories. These differences are typically most apparent in homes with stay-at-home fathers because such men are among the rare fathers who are as involved in parenting as are most mothers. But even in homes where mothers are the primary caregivers, today's more involved fathers have demonstrated their own uniquely effective parenting practices. For the first time in history, it has become possible to directly compare the parenting styles of fathers and mothers in similar settings.

The unique practices of involved fathers, what we call "fatherstyle," are the focus of this book. What exactly is fatherstyle? Let's start with some real-world examples of the differences between the way mothers and fathers parent. Katie, the preteen daughter of stay-at-home father Stephen, chooses to have her mother help her with her homework. Why? "Mom always helps me get the answer, no matter how long it takes. Dad will help me a little, but then he just tells me to figure it out for myself."

Eric, an involved father of two, gets frustrated because his wife Janet has so much trouble getting their children to follow her directions. "I just tell them what to do, and they do it. But Janet asks them, over and over, and they just ignore her. Then, instead of punishing them, she talks to them about how it makes her feel when they ignore her."

Both of these examples illustrate some of the fundamental ways in which fathers and mothers differ in their approach to parenting. We've reduced these differences to five elements which together constitute fatherstyle, a playactive, expectation-oriented approach that helps children develop their emotional and intellectual gifts to grow into independent, happy, and productive adults. The five elements of *fatherstyle* are as follows:

1. *Playactivity*
2. *Independence*
3. *Discipline*
4. *Emotional Intelligence*
5. *Expectation*

In the pages that follow we show clearly and specifically how mothers *and* fathers can use the five elements of fatherstyle to dramatically improve their happiness and effectiveness as parents.

Now that we have set out the elements of fatherstyle, let's revisit the definition of *the fatherstyle advantage* we provided in the introduction. The fatherstyle advantage refers to those things that fathers do best when it comes to parenting and to the extra edge that children get from the way dads raise them differently: an extra edge that makes them more likely to grow into happy, successful adults. In the remainder of the book we will make it plain that fatherstyle parenting can make a positive, lasting difference for mothers, fathers, and their children.

A Sound Basis in Research

While we are the first to coin the term "fatherstyle," we are not the first to note that there are a number of uniquely effective parenting practices that involved fathers tend to employ. Indeed, the overwhelming evidence that supports the existence of fatherstyle and the important benefits it offers for parents and children alike has been around for some time.

For example, many, perhaps most, people still take it for granted that mothers are biologically hard-wired to be better parents than fathers. Surveys consistently show that overwhelming majorities of Americans, including involved fathers themselves, believe that women are *naturally* better suited to parenting. Incredibly, this attitude is prevalent even among men who act as primary caregivers for their children!

Kevin: I was dumbfounded a couple of years ago when I was serving on a parenting panel with several other at-home dads. Someone asked us whether we believed that women were naturally better at parenting. I was the only one who said no!

Jim: Why did these dads think that women had some natural advantage?

Kevin: I don't know. They didn't cite any evidence. It made me realize how deeply ingrained the notion has become. I suppose that most people consider it so obvious they don't need any evidence.

But clinical and social research *long ago* established that there is no scientific basis for the widely-held view that women are somehow naturally better parents than men. Michael Lamb, a respected authority on child development, declares that "[s]ocial convention, not biological imperatives, underlie the traditional division of parental responsibilities." He concludes that "[w]ith the exception of lactation, there is no evidence that women are biologically predisposed to be better parents than men."

Professor Lamb's findings are backed up by dozens of other researchers. For example, Ross Parke and Armin Brott cite the experiences of other cultures:

There's no question that throughout history, fathers have taken on less of the care and feeding of infants and young children than mothers. It would be a mistake, however, to conclude that this is true because mothers have some sort of biologically based nurturing or caretaking superiority. If so, one might expect fathers in all cultures to play a relatively minor role in childcare. But this is not the case. Fathers in a number of other countries share infant and childcare more or less equally with their wives . . . . Clearly, the family roles played by mothers and fathers are not biologically fixed. Instead, they vary with prevailing social, ideological, and other conditions.

But the venerable stereotype that mothers are biologically superior as parents persists despite the growing body of sociological research demonstrating the opposite.

Beyond Mr. Mom

There are approximately three million stay-at-home fathers in the United States today, double the number twenty years ago. And this number does not include single fathers. Of course, these men represent a tremendous variety of situations and experiences. There are as many types of full-time fathers as there are full-time mothers. Many men become stay-at-home fathers because they have lost their jobs. Others stay at home only while their children are very young, returning to the work force when their children enter school. Still others, like Kevin, are full-time fathers by choice and have no firm plans to resume full-time work until their children are in college.

The phenomenon of stay-at-home dads has now become an undeniable part of American popular culture. The idea of full-time fathers first entered the national consciousness via the 1983 film *Mr. Mom* starring Michael Keaton and Teri Garr as parents forced to switch roles when the husband is laid off. After a series of misadventures chronicling his amusing attempts to adjust to running a household with three young children, Keaton's character eventually manages to handle the role on his own terms.

While *Mr. Mom* is unquestionably light and enjoyable entertainment, the term "Mr. Mom" has since taken on a meaning entirely independent of the film. It's become a sort of national shorthand for any father who finds himself taking care of his children without his wife around, for whatever reason, whether for a single afternoon or years on end. Many full-time fathers find the term Mr. Mom insulting. After all, they reason, working mothers are never referred to as "Mrs. Dad." Such a term would instantly be recognized as an offensive put-down, because it would imply that there is something unnatural, or at least less than feminine, about a mother who works.

Does the moniker Mr. Mom imply that a man is less than masculine? Perhaps, but it is worth noting that the character Michael Keaton plays in the film *Mr. Mom* undergoes tremendous personal growth as a result of his accidental role change (his wife, does, too). In the end, not only is he great at running the house and handling the kids, but he is a better person, too. So much so that when he is offered his old job back he agrees to return only on the condition that he can work part-time. You see, he wants to spend more time raising his kids.

It is now clear that stay-at-home dads are here to stay. Their numbers may never make them a majority, or even a significant percentage, of fathers, but their influence has been profound. Whether they are called stay-at-home dads, full-time fathers, or even Mr. Moms, they have changed the face of fatherhood forever by helping all of us to realize that fathers can contribute a lot more to their families than a paycheck. And in many neighborhoods they serve as a daily reminder that parenthood is not the exclusive province of moms.

There's much more. Over forty years ago psychologist Robert Sears led a study of the parenting practices of several hundred parents of five-year-olds. His purpose was to determine the level of empathy in the children and what effect differing parenting styles had on it. Much later another research project tracked down the children from the Sears study and measured their empathy level as adults. They concluded that the most important factor in determining an adult's level of empathy was the amount of paternal involvement at age five.

Another follow-up a decade later confirmed that those adults with the happiest and healthiest personal relationships were those who had the most nurturing relationships with their fathers when they were five years old. Dr. Sears's research thus sparked interest in a field that had not even existed through the immediate postwar period: the importance of involved fathers to children's development.

Ask psychologists about the seminal work on the importance of involved fathers and they will point with virtual unanimity to Michael Lamb's *The Role of the Father in Child Development,* now in its third edition. Dr. Lamb is now happy to point out how many young fathers expect to be actively involved parents, but when he set out to document the importance of involved fathers such men were few and far between. His work has been built upon by the many excellent researchers and authors who have continued to document just how influential fathers can be in the lives of their children.

Another pioneer researcher was Norma Radin, Professor at the University of Michigan. Dr. Radin conducted decades of research on children with involved fathers and found that those youngsters who scored highest in a variety of developmental categories were those with active dads. Her widely-quoted conclusion? "The evidence is quite robust that kids who have contact with a father have an advantage over kids without that kind of contact."

Dr. Ross Parke of the University of California Riverside's Center for Family Studies conducted his own groundbreaking research on the development of social behavior in young children beginning in the late 1960s. Parke established that new fathers, when given the opportunity, exhibit behavior that is just as nurturing as new mothers. He thus helped prove that women are not naturally superior parents than men.

More important, Parke was the first researcher to specifically document differences in mother/father parenting styles and posit that the typical father's approach can have advantages over that of mothers. Indeed, so dramatic were his findings that his graduate student assistants took to wearing T-shirts declaring that "Fathers Make Better Mothers." While Parke understood the sentiment, he never set out to prove that fathers are better parents. Rather, his work has been directed at showing how fathers' involvement is fundamentally important for children's healthy social development.

A pioneer worthy of special note is Kyle Pruett. Author of *Fatherneed: Why Father Care Is as Essential as Mother Care for Your Child,* Pruett is a medical doctor who has conducted more than twenty-five years of acclaimed clinical research at the Yale Child Study Center. His work has gone a long way to establishing that what he terms "engaged fathering" is important to children's well-being. Pruett is a frequent keynote speaker at conferences and seminars devoted to involved fatherhood and he is an unfailingly articulate advocate for the important role men can play as parents. His studies of stay-at-home fathers and their children demonstrate that fathers are just as capable as mothers when it comes to full-time child rearing. Pruett's work has even established that fathers can do a better job of helping children to develop the emotional and intellectual qualities they need to become happy, successful adults.

In each of the remaining chapters of the book we will discuss this research in greater detail and explain how it can serve as the basis for a new approach to the challenges of parenting. And while the term "fatherstyle" is our own invention, it would not be possible to talk about what all parents can learn from today's most involved fathers without the groundwork laid by this research over the last fifty years.

The Limits of Fatherstyle

We believe strongly in the power of fatherstyle to help mothers and fathers improve their parenting. But we want to leave you with two thoughts as you begin to read about fatherstyle in detail. First, fatherstyle is not a one-stop solution to all of the parenting problems affecting millions of individual families.

Conflicting Views

There are (at least) two sides to every story, and the debate over the role of fathers in parenting is no exception. There is a great deal of competing research on the parenting differences between men and women. While our book is written for a popular audience and we have no desire to conduct a point-by-point refutation of those who disagree with our premises, we do want to comment on one book that summarizes the most common competing claims.

In their thoughtful book *Same Difference: How Gender Myths Are Hurting Our Relationships, Our Children, and Our Jobs*, Rosalind Barnett and Caryl Rivers cite research demonstrating that men who assume the role of primary caregiver for their children end up parenting just like mothers. They refer to "a major study of fathers" that found that men who actually took care of their kids on more than a casual basis underwent a transformation. They developed "maternal thinking," and became "sensitive and nurturing caregivers."

This stereotypical language serves to point out the bias of the researchers involved: by defining nurturing behavior as "maternal" they unsurprisingly conclude that involved fathers have nothing unique to offer: instead, they simply act like mothers. We maintain, however, that good parenting is not necessarily "maternal," and that mothers certainly do not have a monopoly on good parenting.

Barnett and Rivers also cite a 1991 review of thousands of studies purporting to find that mothers and fathers do not parent differently in categories defined by seven key markers. Since that study, however, more specific research has established that fathers *do* parent differently when they have the opportunity to serve as primary caregivers. Moreover, none of the studies cited addresses the experiences of millions of involved fathers who are proving every day that they are uniquely competent. As we will note throughout the book, the true test of fatherstyle has not been in a clinical setting but in the many homes across America in which involved fathers are blazing their own parenting trail.

Significantly, all of the research establishes that fathers are just as capable of being good parents as are mothers. Whether one concludes that fathers parent differently than mothers may depend more on one's own stereotypes regarding what constitutes good parenting than on clinical results. But by defining all good parenting practices as "maternal," even the most careful researchers suggest the false conclusion that involved fathers have nothing special to offer.

Like a diet that lets you eat anything you like and never exercise, such a solution simply does not exist. Fatherstyle is but one tool that parents can use to confront the many unique challenges they face in today's rapidly changing world. Of course, we believe that it is a tool that is exceptionally effective and easy to use; we wouldn't have written this book if we believed otherwise. Nevertheless, we will take pains throughout the book not to exaggerate the potential of fatherstyle, and we advise you to do the same.

Second, every parent has his or her own unique personality and style. While we all have room for improvement, none of us can parent just like someone else—nor should we. Our purpose is not to eliminate your own parenting style and replace it with fatherstyle. On the contrary, our hope is that you will learn to understand the elements of fatherstyle and naturally incorporate our approach into the way you parent. After all, what makes you a truly special parent is what you bring along on the journey, not what you pick up along the way.

2

The Power of Play

Using Playactivity to Stimulate Children's Development

"Play is the work of children."

—Anonymous

Kevin: I can't count the number of times I've witnessed the same scene when I'm at the park or playground with my children. A father will be there with his kids, chasing them, pushing them high on the swings, throwing them in the air and catching them, watching them climb to the highest part of the play equipment. And a few feet away, several mothers looking on in horror. Absolutely transfixed. So paralyzed with fear that they cannot even call 911 on their cell phones, these mothers are waiting for the inevitable terrible injury and trip to the emergency room. I've never seen anyone get hurt, but that doesn't make the mothers feel any better. It just convinces them that there is certain to be a catastrophe the next time.

If you asked people to describe what separates the way fathers and mothers parent, most would mention how they play. They might point out that fathers tend to be more physical and unpredictable when playing with their children. This view matches the experience of most families.

According to Dr. Ross Parke, a pioneering researcher on the importance of fathers and author of *Throwaway Dads,* "[t]he area in which fathers' parenting style is most obvious and most important is play." As we will see later in this chapter, Parke's extensive research has revealed that fathers engage in a special, uniquely stimulating kind of play with their children. We call this different approach "playactivity," and it is a central feature of fatherstyle. Indeed, playactivity is so important to fatherstyle that it forms the underpinning for virtually everything that follows in this book.

In this chapter we will talk about what constitutes play and playactivity, why it is vital for children's healthy development, and tell you about practical steps all parents can take to become more playactive.

Defining Play

What is play? The question seems so simple that it is almost embarrassing to ask. But contrary to what most people think, play consists of much more than babies stacking blocks or a gradeschoolers' game of baseball. In his outstanding book *Playful Parenting,* Lawrence Cohen notes that "older children define play as whatever you do with your friends. However, toddlers and preschoolers define play as doing whatever you choose." Parenting expert William Sears writes that "[b]asically play is doing, rather than watching." For Sears, play involves the senses—hearing, feeling, seeing. Play at its best offers choices, possibilities, different ways to explore a problem.

Play really means whatever children do when they are not sleeping or being directed by adults, when they are following their own imaginations and unique directions. Playing with blocks or trucks are classic forms of play for very young children. So is a pickup ballgame or a round of Monopoly for older children.

Play changes depending on a child's age. Teachers speak of "parallel play" when they refer to toddlers and preschoolers. This describes the mode of play in which children play in the same room, but not together. Later, preschoolers learn how to play cooperatively. As children grow, their play naturally becomes more organized. They may act out familiar scenarios such as cops and robbers or pretend to be a superhero. Even later, they will prefer play with increasingly elaborate rules such as board games or team sports.

Whether they realize it or not, most children are playing most of the time. Of course, adults play, too. Sometimes we play the same games as we did when we were children. Other times we make up new games or enjoy watching others play well. Indeed, it is impossible for most of us to imagine a life devoid of play.

The Importance of Play

Play is fun, but it also has a serious side. Play is a child's means of connecting with the world. And while different children play differently, and styles of play naturally change as children grow, it always remains central to their healthy emotional and physical growth. Cohen calls play "children's main way of communicating, of experimenting, of learning." It is not an exaggeration to state that play is the foundation for everything that comes later. Research on play reveals that children who are good at play tend to develop into happier, better-adjusted adults. Children who are deprived of good play experiences, by contrast, are substantially more likely to suffer from difficulties later in life.

We are all instinctively aware of the importance of play in children's lives. When we think of a child experiencing problems, we immediately picture a child alone, perhaps staring into the distance. Psychologists know that children who are unable to play are typically in emotional pain. Similarly, children will often communicate emotional difficulties via play rather than words. Child psychologists and psychotherapists who work with children find that play and games help children reveal what they are feeling but cannot express in words.

What specifically is so important about play? Cohen identifies three main functions of play for children: play helps children develop *confidence and mastery* of the world around them; play helps foster *close emotional bonds*; and play helps children *recover from emotional distress*. Let's briefly examine each of these functions in turn.

Confidence and Mastery

It's easy for adults to forget that children have very few opportunities to exercise power in their lives. One undeniable feature of play is that children typically get to direct it themselves: they decide *when* to play, *what* to play, and they even get to assign roles, often to the very adults who boss them around all day. No wonder children love to play so much!

As Cohen points out, this self-determination is part of the power aspect of play. Power is exercised on several levels. The most fundamental is that the children get to be the boss. More important, play provides children with a sense of mastery of the world around them. Not only do they get to direct other people and events, but they also have an opportunity to practice new roles through repetition.

For toddlers, a sense of mastery is vital. All parents understand how toddlers need to enjoy a feeling of safety and protection while simultaneously enjoying opportunities to develop independence and competence. Play is central to the development of mastery, particularly in very young children.

When does mastery take place? When a child is permitted to test his abilities without becoming overwhelmed. Lieberman describes the process as follows: "Mastery is possible when the child's capacities are tested but not overwhelmed by the challenge. If, on the other hand, the parents are overly lenient and try to spare the child the necessary developmental frustrations, she will grow unsure of her coping skills and may become anxious in the face of even minor trials and tribulations."

On a simpler level, children can *make things happen* when they play. Play provides them with opportunities to experience feelings of power and competence. Just like their junior counterparts, older children also experience confidence and mastery through play. While their activities are more sophisticated, often involving complicated rules and the dynamics of team interaction, the fundamentals remain the same. Indeed, one of the great selling points of sports and other forms of organized play for older children is that they build confidence.

Close Emotional Bonds

It is obvious that play, like any activity in which people spend time with their children, can foster emotional bonds. In *Raising a Secure Child,* Zeynep

Biringen, Ph.D., calls play "[o]ne of the best ways in which emotional connection (or reconnection) can happen."

For very young children, these bonds involve mom and dad. Indeed, this is so central to play that many of the most popular games for infants and toddlers involve testing emotional connection by experimenting with parental absence. Think about peekaboo. A baby playing this game with his father or mother is learning about absence, specifically that someone can seem to go away and come back. Even though babies cannot yet understand that an out-of-sight object still exists, they are fascinated by the game.

Now consider hide-and-seek. This is a popular game among toddlers and especially preschoolers. Hide-and-seek is simply a more sophisticated form of peekaboo. It's all about testing the implications of relational distance. Parents learn quickly that children can become very emotional during hide-and-seek. Stay hidden too long and many children will become upset and even begin to panic. But if you hide in an easy place a child may get frustrated because you're not far enough away!

For school-age children, hide-and-seek becomes a game they play with their friends. It helps them negotiate the new terrain of friendship. Tag is also popular for the same reason. All of these games are about splitting apart and coming back together, a fundamental emotional theme for all children. Playing helps children express their emotions and learn how to deal with them in a safe and fun setting.

Cohen speculates that the reason older children describe play as "something you do with your friends" is that they understand the function of play as a way of building emotional closeness. We all understand this. After all, what is likely to cause more parental worry than a comment from the teacher that a child does not play with other children during recess? Whether the situation is the result of the child's own choice or that of his classmates, it is a legitimate cause for concern precisely because play is the primary way that children relate to other people. If they're not playing, chances are they're not relating.

Indeed, play is so important in this regard that you cannot be an involved, loving parent if you do not play often with your children. Biringen writes that "[t]hrough playing, parents can begin to learn about a child's internal world—the world that he or she might not be able to reveal in other ways."

Emotional Recovery

With rare exceptions, we don't usually think of children as suffering from emotional traumas. But the truth is that children, like adults, suffer emotional hurts every day. They may not rise to the level of a trauma by our grown-up standards, but they can nevertheless be quite traumatic to children. We can laugh now about how upset we were when the dog chewed on our favorite toy or when the teacher scolded us in front of the rest of the class, but those events caused very real injury at the time.

How do adults recover from emotional injuries? In a variety of ways, but commonly by engaging in an activity we particularly enjoy or by talking it over with someone we trust. For young children, of course, talking it over is typically out of the question. As parents of teenagers know all too well, even older children often find it difficult to discuss emotional hurts.

That's where play comes in. Often children can recover from emotional traumas through play alone. Older children can use play as an opening to learn how to talk about their feelings. Play permits children to recover by engaging in a favorite activity.

Lieberman states that "[p]lay is a major avenue for learning to manage anxiety. It gives the child a safe place where he can experiment at will, suspending the rules and constraints of physical and social reality." She notes that the famed psychologist Erik Erikson proposed that play is the way in which children create model situations to experiment with controlling reality. Children overcome emotional difficulties by "playing it out" just as adults do so by "talking it out."

For example, a child may deal with the anxiety of witnessing a loud argument between her parents by acting out a similar situation with her stuffed animals. In the child's version, however, there is a happy ending: the toys hug and promise not to fight anymore. It is no accident that child psychologists often advise parents whose young children are experiencing separation anxiety to use peekaboo and hide-and-seek as tools to overcome the problem.

How Fathers Play Differently

In *Fatherneed,* Kyle Pruett declares that "[t]he father as play partner is one of the most enduring findings in the research on the role of the father in child development." And recall the quote from Ross Parke that opened this chapter: "The area in which fathers' parenting style is most obvious and most important is play."

In everyday life as well the identification of fathers and play is a natural one. Cohen says that when he speaks to parents about play, "someone always says 'I don't really play much with my children; that's more my husband's job.'"

Jim: In all my work with children and their families, I rarely hear from a woman who is the primary play partner with her children. Even most single mothers tend to see play as something outside of their realm of expertise or responsibility.

We can hear many of you responding that mothers don't play as much with their children because they are too busy tackling a disproportionate share of all the myriad household chores. Certainly it's true that mothers still handle a much larger share of the work associated with running a home than do their husbands. But it is far from the whole explanation for fathers' unique role in playing with their children.

When asked what is different about fathers' play, most people will point to the fact that fathers tend to be more physical. "Roughhousing" is the term that is heard most often, what used to be called "horsing around" not so long ago. That is certainly one aspect of fathers' play. But there are others. According to David Popenoe of Rutgers University, "[a]t play and in other realms, fathers tend to stress competition, challenge, initiative, risk-taking, and independence."

We have isolated four hallmarks of fathers' play with children: it is *physical, exploratory, silly,* and *challenging*. Let's discuss each of these features in turn. We refer to them collectively as *playactivity*.

Physical Playactivity

Pruett notes that "scientific observations have identified . . . a common paternal behavior: the predisposition in fathers to enjoy activating their children in order to interact with them." They do so from the very beginning by being robustly physical, picking up their children, swinging and bouncing them, and rolling around on the floor with them. According to Parke, "[a]nyone who has ever watched new parents in action can attest that women tend to play more visual games with their babies and are often more verbal with them. Men, on the other hand, are far more physical, right from the time their kids are infants."

Specific research confirms this pattern. The celebrated pediatrician T. Berry Brazelton and his colleague Michael Yogman observed how parents and strangers played with two-week-old and six-month-old infants. They found that mothers tended to engage with their children by speaking in soothing tones, often repeating comforting phrases and the baby's own sounds. The researchers documented what they termed a "burst-pause" pattern, in which mothers repeated phrases and sounds and were then silent. Fathers, by contrast, engaged with their infants by being less verbal and more physical. They touched their babies more, even when they were lying in their cribs, rhythmically stroking or tapping. Fathers tended to engage their infants intensely and then withdraw, versus the gradual shifting in attention that characterized the mothers' interactions.

The responses of the involved fathers we interviewed provide additional support for fathers' emphasis on physical play. Dave told a vivid story of how he and his daughter used to play wild physical games around the house while mom was at work all day. "We'd trash the whole place and then clean it up before Cathy got home," Dave said. "Once I videotaped the house before we cleaned just so she could see what it looked like. She was appalled, claiming that I would 'hurt' Molly. In fact, my wife was always afraid she'd get hurt." Bernard told of wrestling games with his three boys after dinner, including games in which they would try to "push back" and topple their father.

The reasons for fathers' devotion to physical play are unclear. Pruett speculates that fathers seek out a physical connection with their infants because they are so physically disconnected from the process of pregnancy and birth. Whatever the reason, there is no question that most fathers of young children are much more intensely physical in their play than are most mothers.

Brazelton concluded that "[m]ost fathers tend to present a more playful, jazzing-up approach. As one watches the interaction, it seems that a father is expecting more heightened, playful response from the baby. And he gets it!" Pruett calls this process of jazzing up "activation," and it is a phenomenon that appears throughout the research on differences in the parenting styles of mothers and fathers.

Exploratory Playactivity

Parke has observed that "fathers . . . tend to allow their infants more freedom to explore, while mothers are usually more cautious. Fathers also encourage their children's independence by promoting exploration." Fathers' play style also tends to be unpredictable. Pruett writes that "[f]ather play also tends to be qualitatively different from mother play in that it is frequently nonconventional. It relies less on traditional games and themes and more on the activation-exploration theme."

How is this reflected in the way fathers play with their children? Fathers are more likely to permit, and even encourage, their children to find things out for themselves. Fathers will place an infant on the floor and watch as she examines the world. They are slower to intervene when children become confused, frustrated, or frightened. They insist that children try new approaches and practice unfamiliar behaviors. In Chapter 3 we'll talk about how fathers excel at encouraging their children's independence throughout their lives.

Fathers also tend to play less with toys, improvising play using readily available objects and materials. A classic father-child interaction involves doing jobs around the house. The child is designated as a "helper" or "assistant" and does her job by handing tools to dad, asking probing questions, and suggesting solutions to tough problems.

Silly Playactivity

There's something about dads and wacky behavior. Perhaps because they often think of themselves as just big kids themselves, fathers seem to have an easier time behaving in unconventional, even silly ways with their children. Parenting writer Carolyn Hoyt noted that "[o]ne aspect of child rearing in which dads seem to excel effortlessly is showing their babies a good time." And Armin Brott has written that dads often get off the beaten path when it comes to modifying games, creating wacky family rituals, and making ordinary everyday activity extraordinary.

Challenging Playactivity

While competition is something only older children understand, fathers' emphasis on challenge, initiative, risk-taking, and independence starts from the time their children are infants. For example, fathers are less likely to do things for their children or to step in and solve their problems for them. Research demonstrates that mothers step in to spare their children the frustration that comes with learning a new task. Fathers are more content to watch and help their children deal with the emotions that come with frustration rather than completing the task for them.

The challenging aspect of playactivity is something that tends to develop as children get older. We'll explore this in more detail later in this chapter.

The Benefits of Playactivity

Parke observes that children "generally respond more positively to play with their fathers than with their mothers." When they are given the choice, more than two-thirds of two-and-a-half-year-olds choose to play with their fathers instead of their mothers. What are children getting from playing with their fathers that is so important to them? Popenoe declares that "[t]he way fathers play affects everything from the management of emotions to intelligence and academic achievement. It is particularly important in promoting the essential virtue of self-control."

Studies show that physical play helps children develop the social skills they need to get along well with their peers. This is because children who roughhouse with an adult learn how to control their impulses. Professor John Snarey of Emory University says that "while they're roughhousing with their fathers, infants are already learning some valuable lessons in self-control." This occurs because children learn to recognize the emotional cues of others. More basically, they also learn early what types of behavior are off limits: hitting, biting, kicking, and scratching.

Cohen agrees that children wrestle and roughhouse as a way of testing out their physical strength, as a way to have fun, and as a way to control their aggression. Significantly, he believes that physical play benefits all types of children:

> *Boys and girls—rambunctious children and quiet ones—all benefit from thoughtful physical play with adults. The active ones, who are going to be in the thick of the rough and tumble in school and on the playground, need a chance to do it first with someone who can give them undivided attention, help them deal with their fears, hesitations, impulses, anger, etc. . . . Meanwhile, children who are less physically active need roughhousing with adults so they can explore their physical power and develop their confidence and assertiveness.*

Kevin: Don't you think a lot of mothers are surprised at the violent and aggressive play of their toddlers and preschoolers?

Jim: I do think that. It seems to come as a complete shock for many mothers—and a few fathers, too—that their young children, especially their boys, would behave in an aggressive manner.

Kevin: Is it because mothers don't understand boys?

Jim: I think that's part of it at times. If a woman has not grown up with brothers, particularly younger brothers, she may not have witnessed this aggression first-

hand. What women see as normal may be related to how they were as children.

Kevin: I wonder, too, if there's just less knowledge about child development among young parents in general.

Jim: That's a good point. Some surveys of parents of young children have shown that many parents (and this includes both mothers and fathers) simply do not know what to expect of toddlers and preschoolers.

Kevin: From my own experience, I can assure parents that a lot of boys will be aggressive.

Jim: I can do the same. Boys are inclined to be more aggressive in their play and life will be easier for parents if they understand this before they are broadsided by it.

The lesson of aggression control may have special value for boys. Fathers usually rise to the occasion by helping their preschool-age sons displace and discharge their aggression and anxious rivalry by engaging them in physical play. William Pollack, celebrated author of *Real Boys: Rescuing Our Sons from the Myths of Boyhood* and professor at the Harvard Medical School, says that fathers' playactivity has special benefits for boys, who learn "how to engage in a broad range of appropriately spirited behaviors."

Girls benefit, too. Armin Brott, author of *Father for Life* and a popular series of fathering books, notes that research shows that girls do better in school, career, and relationships when they grow up playing physically with their dads. Dave, the father we met earlier, notes that he made a conscious decision to emphasize physical play with his nine-year-old daughter to teach her "that she's tough and she can take on any boy." He feels that it's especially important to teach resilience to girls, helping them to learn from experience that "problems are what give you personality."

Physical play has other benefits for all children. Cohen cites several things that children learn through physical play with their parents, including self-soothing (the ability to comfort and calm yourself without assistance), paying attention, motor planning and sequencing (organizing tasks and following through in a timely fashion), and impulse control.

That's not all. Christopher Brown, vice president for national programming at the National Fatherhood Initiative, notes that "[p]hysical play with dad encourages risk-taking and independence. Kids see dad as the biggest, smartest, and strongest guy around. Having such a positive role model fosters confidence and security."

Research also establishes that children who get along best with other children are more likely to have fathers who spend a lot of time playing physically with them. Moreover, children who have good play relationships with their fathers also tend to have better, longer-lasting friendships as they grow. These children typically need less guidance from adults in handling the difficult emotions and choices of adolescence.

Perhaps most startling, fathers' skills as playmates are excellent predictors of their children's intellectual development. In other words, fathers who are the best playmates often have the smartest children. Why is this? Some experts suggest that fathers' unconventional play style helps children develop greater creativity and faith in themselves, not to mention willingness to take intellectual risks.

When kids are school age, the nature of their play changes, and then it is usually Dad who introduces them to games, competition, and the rules of play. This kind of play involves a special kind of intellectual stimulation which is helpful in children's cognitive development. Girls in particular benefit from this altered emphasis. Studies find that girls whose fathers play with them are more assertive in their interpersonal relationships throughout their lives and more successful as adults.

How to Become a Playactive Parent

All of our talk about the importance of play and how fathers' playactive style contributes to children's healthy development is well and good, but it would amount to little more than interesting academic discourse without some plan for parents to put it into practice themselves. Fortunately, we've developed such a plan. In the remainder of this chapter we'll outline the eight essentials

The Benefits of Laughter

Laughter itself is beneficial. Dr. Louis Franzini notes in his book *Kids Who Laugh: How To Develop Your Child's Sense of Humor*, that laughter "is one of the most desirable personality traits." He writes that a sense of humor is important to developing social skills, not to mention problem-solving abilities. Research demonstrates that a healthy sense of humor can help children avoid physical and emotional problems later in life.

Laughter can also help overcome some tough situations. Libby Gill relates the story of a father whose son suffered a black eye while they were sledding, an activity his mother felt was too dangerous. His father told the boy to respond "You oughta see the other guy," when they got home as a way of defusing his mother's reaction to the injury. She noted that the father "fostered his own special brand of humor to soften the cuts, scrapes, and bruises of Jimmy's life."

You can make a conscious effort to help your children develop a healthy sense of humor. Many of the things we already mention in our discussion of silly play will accomplish this goal. There are other things you can do, too, particularly with older children, who can be a tough audience. Get a joke book out of the library and write comedy routines that you try out on a family joke night ("ahem . . . is this thing on?").

Make sure to poke fun at yourself every now and then. Cohen suggests doing something unexpected: "The unexpected response is a basic technique of comedy, both in the theater and at home. So don't go into your preteen's room to tell her, for the tenth time, to clean it. Go in and scream, 'Girl Power!' and sing a current pop song (complete with dancing, of course). If you don't get a laugh, at least she might say 'Okay, okay, I'll clean my room, just please never do that again!'"

Kevin: I actually tried this with my eight-year-old daughter, and it got a goofy laugh (although I couldn't sing a popular song because I didn't know any).

Jim: I always used a lot of sarcasm in trying to get my stepson to clean up his room, suggesting that the health department might visit and arrest me.

Remember that every child, like every adult, has a different sense of humor. You need to get to know your children a bit before you can predict what will work with each of them (see how this all fits together?).

Kevin: I always get a laugh when I tell my daughter I'm coming to one of her choral concerts with her brothers wearing T-shirts and waving flags with her name on them. "Oh, Dad," she says, "you wouldn't really do that, would you?" My six-year-old son, however, would be thrilled if I did that at his class show.

Be prepared to do some experimenting and adjust your routine accordingly. Who knows, you might have a future on *Saturday Night Live*.

of playactivity and describe steps all mothers and fathers can take to incorporate these elements into their parenting every day.

The Eight Essentials of Playactivity

Earlier we discussed what fathers do differently that constitutes playactivity: Fatherstyle play is *physical, exploratory, silly,* and *challenging*. Now we'll get more specific and describe the types of play that best exemplify these features.

The Eight Essentials of Playactivity are:

1. *Time* for Play
2. *Floor* Play
3. *Physical* Play
4. *Following* Play
5. *Go-Between* Play
6. *Verbal* Play
7. *Silly* Play
8. *Exploratory* Play

At the end of this section we will present a Playactivity Chart summarizing the elements of playactivity and what parents can do to become more playactive at each stage of their children's lives.

Make Time for Play

The necessary first step to becoming a playactive parent is, of course, making time for play. Many parents believe that this is an impossibility given their busy family schedules, but remember that many fathers with demanding, full-time jobs still manage to find the time to play with their children.

What does this involve? It is *not* taking your child to the playground and letting your child play, or arranging playdates, or taking your child to preschool and making sure he or she has an opportunity to play. It means actually *playing* with your child.

We recommend scheduling a half-hour a day for playtime. Without one-on-one play, it is tough to get to know your child's likes and dislikes. That half-hour a day would be the most desired slot of time for your child, so set up the emotional connection by arranging regular playtimes. You may even find it useful to create a list of fun activities you can engage in with each of your children every day. You can then consult the list instead of spending time wondering what to do.

Even if you can't schedule that much time, you can still play with your child regularly. Try doing your household activities in a playful way. Have fun at the breakfast table or create a regular end-of-the-day game. Bathtime and bedtime are a natural time for some (quiet) play. Even a few minutes of play will mean a lot to your children.

Get on the Floor

You can't really play unless you go where your child is: the floor. A surprising number of parents never get on the floor with their children; they probably believe that play is something children do alone or with other children only. In order to get physical, you must get on the floor. You may get a better perspective when you see things from your child's point of view.

For young children, floor play typically involves crawling around, playing peekaboo, or stacking blocks. Toddlers and preschoolers will enjoy building large puzzles, playing tickle games, working with more complicated blocks, hide-and-seek, and trying some simple board games. School-age children will have fun with more physical games, such as wrestling, as well as complicated board games, puzzles, and card games.

Get Physical

As we've already noted, physicality is the hallmark of playactivity. Contrary to popular thought, you can be very physical even with infants. Touching, carrying, moving limbs and digits, and swinging (carefully) are all ways you can play physically with your infant. Perhaps the popularity of infant massage reflects a growing recognition of how babies crave touching. Touching your child stimulates his senses and shows him how much you love him. Roll him around, tickle his feet, swing him, and bounce him on your knee.

With toddlers and preschoolers, physical play means swinging, tossing, and running around games such as hide-and seek or just chase. Of course, you must be very sensitive to your child's state of mind. It's very easy for them to become overstimulated or even scared when playing this way.

Jim: Some children can be overstimulated by a physical brand of play, but I find it a matter of timing, don't you?

Kevin: Sure. For example, getting your child stimulated just before bedtime is not a good idea. There should be a winding down before bedtime—not a revving up.

This is also a great age to start using physical play to confront emotional or behavioral issues. Many parents facing bedtime struggles with their young children find that turning bedtime into a physical game (not too physical, of course, or you'll overagitate your child) can make the process easier.

Kevin: With my own two boys I made a routine out of a lullaby followed by a one-two-three and a gentle toss into bed. They loved it until their increasing size and my advancing age made it a memory.

What about school-age children? For them, roughhousing is one answer. They're typically large enough that you don't have to worry so much about hurting them, and they're very interested in testing their strength against yours. Lawrence Cohen considers this type of play so important that he devotes an entire chapter of his book *Playful Parenting* to wrestling. He notes at the outset that mothers tend to object to wrestling and often refuse to consider trying it. His suggestion and ours: give the idea a chance "[e]ven if you don't think you ever want to wrestle, or even if you think you already know all about wrestling."

Keep in mind that we're not talking about the kind of wrestling you see on television. Even if it's staged, it can be very dangerous. We mean controlled roughhousing, with a set of rules and adult guidance. Make sure you have a lot of room, and your child understands that he can stop the game whenever he wants. This will give him the combination of danger and control that he is seeking.

As your children get even older, physical play will usually involve sports and outdoor activities. Greg, a father of three children aged nine, eleven, and thirteen, told us that this is his preferred method of play. "I do quite a bit outdoors with my kids. I take walks with them, go fishing, throw the football, and take our dogs for a run." This is a common, and healthy, form of playactivity.

And don't forget organized athletics. Too many of us think we have to be the world's greatest athlete to support our children's physical play. We don't, and what's more, we don't have to become team coaches, either. Just let your child know you're interested in (and proud of) his athletic activities, take time to practice with him in the backyard, and do your best to attend scheduled practices and games.

Don't Lead, Follow

Resist the urge to suggest an activity or direct the play. Hang back as much as you can and let your child show you what she enjoys doing. Then do it. Lieberman advises that "[t]he essence of play is spontaneity, and toddlers know how to do it better than grown-ups do." In other words, you can give permission and can follow your child's lead, but you need to be careful not to interfere with your child's own pace by injecting your agenda about what he should be solving through play.

The surest way to strengthen your connection with your child is to enter his world. Zeynep Biringen writes that "[o]ne of the nicest things a parent can do for a child is to join in play rather than taking over." This means opening the door to pretend play, often referred to as "higher-level play," by making sure that your child has access to appropriate toys and other props. Another technique is to integrate pretend play into your everyday activities. For example, if you have to replace a hinge on the front door, gather your daughter's toy tools and set them out with your own.

When you play with older children, just as when you play with babies, it's important to take your cues from the child. Whether you're learning from your child about the very latest in trendy fashion dolls or enjoying a building session with good old-fashioned wooden blocks, try to enter your child's world. Gain her trust there and she'll be more willing to try activities and games that interest you. Careful observation of your child's play will help you discover how your child learns best and what she is ready to do. Then you can tailor your suggestions for fun and recreation to suit her developmental skills and emerging preferences.

Use a Go-between

Many adults, parents included, are extremely uncomfortable entering the world of children. They've been in the grownup world for so long that they can't seem to remember how to loosen up! If you find yourself in this situation, try using a stuffed toy or puppet as a stand-in. Let the toy do what you can't, making jokes, dancing, or doing other silly things. After a while you'll find that you'll have an easier time doing those things yourself.

Go-between play is good for your child, too. William Sears advises that "young children may be more willing to confide in a favorite doll, a puppet, or even a make-believe friend whom they know will listen and not talk back. . . . Children may express in this kind of play feelings that they are unable to talk about directly."

With older children, a useful go-between may be a real friend. Ask your children what they enjoy doing with their best friends and then incorporate it into your own play. This approach has the twin virtues of teaching you something about what your children enjoy doing and giving you a template for successful play activities. Also consider acting as a facilitator for friend-to-friend interactions. You may find that your middle school-age child doesn't want to go to the movies with you anymore, but she may be delighted to have you take her and a friend out to dinner and a movie. You'll get a chance to spend more time with your child, and you'll gain some valuable insights into who her friends are and how she behaves around them.

Talk Man to Man (or Woman)

Mothers tend to use baby talk with infants even as they grow. Talk to them as equals, using your adult vocabulary and tone, to stimulate their natural verbal ability. Don't talk down to your children. Make up verbal games with rhymes and other word play. We recommend introducing props into your child's playtime. Props are effective tools for encouraging language development because children can imagine, explain, and demonstrate their uses. For example, by playing school, you encourage your child's language development because he or she will use bigger words when pretending to be the teacher.

One other way of helping to build a great vocabulary in your child while increasing their awareness of the world around them is to narrate. That is, when you are with your child (whether walking in the park, riding a bike, or riding in the car), narrate what you're observing. This allows your child to hear you use words, names, and descriptions, and it draws your child's attention to what is going on around her and assists her in beginning to have a better grasp of the world.

You can use a more advanced form of narration with your older children. When you're watching television or out for a drive, casually start a discussion about what you're watching: "Have you guys started studying Abraham Lincoln in school?" Whatever the answer, mention a few important facts on the subject. You'll be surprised at how much they remember later, and you might even stimulate an interest in a subject your child never thought much about before.

Be Silly

One of the great advantages fathers have over mothers is their willingness to act foolish to get attention. They make funny faces, do a strange dance, do anything to energize their play. To our knowledge no one has done any research to determine why mothers are reluctant to engage in such play. In any event, being silly is an important part of becoming a playactive parent.

What's silly? *The unexpected. The disruptive. The different.* Kevin and his wife were at a local parade with their nephew when he was about five years old.

He sat stone-faced as the clowns went by, took no notice of the march of dressed-up dachshunds, and even ignored the colorful floats. But he howled with uncontrollable laughter when a guy dressed as a giant cell phone appeared. The other things were all expected, but the idea of a giant phone walking down the street—now *that's* hilarious.

Being silly is easier said than done, you might argue. Well, yes. Helping someone learn how to be silly is much more challenging than providing tips on how to become a more physical play partner. Some of us find it a lot harder than others to loosen up. Cohen calls the process "losing your dignity with your child." We prefer to think of it as reestablishing contact with your inner child. And it can be a difficult process for many of us.

Nevertheless, there are some specific techniques you can adopt. The basic idea is to be unconventional and do the unexpected. For example, we all know how to make funny faces and sounds when interacting with babies. With toddlers, practicing random acts of silliness, such as making a sandwich with the peanut butter on the outside or insisting that mom and dad must eat with the kids' silverware, are sure-fire hits. Dressing up in funny clothes or dancing around are other good silly activities to try together.

For preschoolers, singing songs with funny lyrics is a favorite, especially if the lyrics are a little naughty. The three Bs—boogers, burps, and butts—are typical crowd pleasers. There are two great books that might help you get started in this regard: *Take Me Out of the Bathtub* and *I'm Still Here in the Bathtub* by Alan Katz. Dancing to great music is another silly possibility for this age group. The albums of Tom Chapin feature great tunes and creative lyrics for all ages.

Still having trouble learning how to be silly? Try the role reversal game. Kevin learned about this while watching a Berenstain Bears video with his kids. In the story, Brother Bear and Sister Bear do a skit at school in which they pretend to be their parents. Kevin's kids found the whole concept so riotous that they begged to play it themselves.

It turns out that the role-reversal game has some sound basis in psychology. Cohen says that the appeal may be that the playing field is leveled, or even tipped a bit in favor of the child, to make up for the frustrations of being smaller and weaker and less competent than the bigger folks. He notes that reversing roles is particularly useful in helping restore children's confidence.

Older children love silly play, too. For school-age children, try the classic game Twister, which incorporates physical play as well as silliness, or word games, such as Pictionary or Scattegories, or simply charades.

Pete's a Pizza

The late William Steig was best known as an illustrator for *The New Yorker* magazine. But many parents and children know that he had another life as an author of imaginative children's books. Steig, who was known as the King of Cartoons, wrote *Shrek!*, the story that led to the astoundingly successful (and very different) film of the same name.

Steig sold his first cartoon to *New Yorker* editor Harold Ross in 1930 and was hired as a staff cartoonist. Over the following seven decades, he produced more than 1,600 drawings and 117 covers for the magazine. He also wrote more than 30 children's books. He began writing children's books when he was 60. His third, *Sylvester and the Magic Pebble*, received the prestigious Caldecott Medal in 1970. Other notable children's books included *Roland, the Minstrel Pig*, *Amos & Boris*, *Doctor De Soto*, and *Wizzil*.

One of Steig's best children's books, however, was *Pete's a Pizza*, written just five years before he died in 2003. This book has particular relevance in the context of our current discussion because it embodies many of the elements of play-activity. In *Pete's a Pizza*, a boy who appears to be about seven or eight years old is in a bad mood because a sudden rainstorm has prevented him from playing ball with his friends. His father comes to the rescue, picking Pete up and pretending to make him into a pizza. The game involves lots of pushing, pulling, and throwing. While Pete's father is pretending to make him into a pizza, his mother stands by with a bemused look on her face. She even joins in a bit after observing for a while. Eventually the father tickles Pete and they play a chasing game until "the pizza gets captured and hugged." Pete's mother then points out that the sun has come out. Pete leaves to look for his friends, his bad mood forgotten.

Pete's a Pizza is a terrific illustration of

Explore

Help your child develop curiosity and confidence by going all around the house seeking out new things. Point them out, touch them, and talk about them. Stop using toys as a crutch. While some toys can be terrific, more often than not they actually inhibit creative play. The exceptions are toys such as simple building blocks and drawing pads.

all of the essential elements of playactivity: the game Pete's father makes up is physical, silly, exploratory, and challenging. The physical and silly features of the game are self-evident. How is the pizza game exploratory? Pete's dad has to come up with creative ways to simulate making his son into a pizza. For example, he rolls him around and pulls on his legs to simulate kneading the dough. He pretends that sprinkled water is olive oil, talcum powder is flour, pieces of paper are cheese, and so on.

How is the game challenging? Pete has to go along with the increasingly silly game, trying his hardest to keep in character. He giggles when his mother says she doesn't like tomatoes on her pizza, but he refuses to answer one of his father's questions "because he's only some dough and stuff." When Pete's mother tickles him and he laughs, his father reminds him that pizzas are not supposed to laugh. Pete responds testily that "pizza-makers are not supposed to tickle their pizzas!" Finally, Pete can't help laughing and he jumps from the table and runs away.

Perhaps most important, the pizza game helps Pete connect with his father (they hug at the end following a chase game) and recover from emotional distress, his bad mood because of the rainstorm. That is, after all, the whole point of the story.

Steig's own comments offer some insight into the mind of this very imaginative and talented man. "I carry on a lot of the functions of an adult but I have to force myself," he said in a 1984 interview with *People* magazine. "For some reason I've never felt grown up." We can all learn a lot from his words. *Pete's a Pizza* is a popular book in Kevin's house, and the pizza game is a perennial favorite as well.

Also do your best to avoid existing scripts when engaging in fantasy play. It's easy for kids to play Batman or SpongeBob because it requires little imagination. The idea of exploratory play, however, is to invent as you go along. Be creative. Make up something brand new and your child will benefit most.

For older children, try a nature walk.

Kevin: We live close to a small nature preserve and every summer I take the kids on a nature hike. I give each of my children a notebook and pencil to record observations and a jumbo reclosable bag filled with many smaller reclosable bags to collect specimens. We finish with a picnic and then discuss their discoveries when we get home. Sometimes it leads to real education as we look up plant types and learn about the forest, but often everything is forgotten as soon as we get home. Either way, it's an adventure and it reminds my children that there's a lot out there they don't understand.

Another good technique is to keep your eye out for interesting activities in your area, particularly those you've never tried before. See a play, visit the science center, even if the subject matter is different than your usual. Not only will you experience some amazing things you would have overlooked otherwise, you will be teaching your children the value of trying new things.

As Children Grow

The importance of playactivity continues throughout childhood. While most of us tend to picture very young children when we think about play, the fact is older children engage in play for more of their typical day than their younger brothers and sisters. Older children still enjoy board games and card games, of course, but as they grow children tend to want to become involved in team activities and organized sports.

Organized athletics can be a tremendous, positive force in the lives of children. They can help children learn about values such as teamwork, perseverance, patience, humility, and, most of all, fairness. Children who have learned about fairness play by the rules, share, take turns, and make sure that the concerns of all have been addressed. Participation in sports can also teach children about the importance of exercise and physical fitness, something that has assumed increasing urgency in light of the epidemic of obesity among America's youth.

Fathers play an important role in imparting these lessons. It's common knowledge that as children become involved in organized sports their fathers tend to be more involved than their mothers. It's no accident that the vast majority of the parents coaching team sports are men. Fathers also tend to spend much more time than mothers practicing sports with their children. In fact, for many older children, their primary contact with their fathers is through activities related to organized sports.

This contact creates a natural opportunity to teach fundamental lessons about coping with the ups and downs of life and getting along with others. Michele Borba recounts the story of a father who taught his hyper-competitive son how to play fairly by teaching him to respect the rules, choose sides by flipping a coin, and showing him how to lose with grace. Curt Schilling, World Series co-MVP pitcher now with the Boston Red Sox, recalls one Little League season when he was upset because he thought the coach wasn't playing him enough. His father told him, "Then it's your job to work harder and become a better player. Make the coach change his mind about you." Curt says, "I've never forgotten that advice." Countless adults today can tell similar stories because their fathers used sports as a means to teach them important lessons about life.

Being a playactive parent means making time to nurture your children's interest in sports of all kinds as they grow. Often this involves developing an intimate knowledge of your children's strengths and weaknesses and likes and dislikes. Indeed, playactive parents learn that it's easier to understand their children's changing personalities when they remain playactive far beyond toddlerhood.

In their book *Good Sports,* Michelle Akers and Gregg Lewis offer some thoughtful guidelines for helping you to make sure your child gets the most out of her participation in sports:

Know Your Child.

Make sure he is playing for good reasons of his own, not just to please you. Ask yourself whether he is physically and emotionally ready to play. Keep tabs on him throughout the season to find out how he's enjoying the experience.

How *Not* to Play

As with everything else when it comes to parenting, involved fathers do not have all the answers. In fact, in preparing this book we came across a number of play-related things that involved fathers tend to do that we specifically discourage. For example, mothers often complain that fathers' "activation" of their children occurs at the wrong times—just before bedtime, or when they're supposed to be doing their homework or cleaning up.

Perhaps it's more of a working parent thing. We heard the same complaint from the stay-at-home dads we interviewed. In her book *Stay-at-Home Dads: The Essential Guide to Creating the New Family*, Libby Gill relates the frustration of Doug, a full-time father with an eleven-month-old son. "One thing that would drive me crazy was when Erin came home from work. She would want to play with Sean, which I understood, but she would hype him up when she should have been winding him down for bedtime." Their solution was to have Erin get up an hour earlier to spend time with Sean before she went to work rather than trying to squeeze playtime in before bedtime in the evening. In short, make sure that you are being responsive to the situation and your children's needs when you are becoming playactive.

Another no-no is playing with the kids by making them do what you want to do. Recall that one of our recommendations for becoming a more playactive parent was to let your child direct the play. Sadly, many fathers (typically those that are not as involved as the ones we portray in this book) don't play with their children. Instead, they insist that the children play with them. This might mean watching sports on television or attending sporting events together. It could also mean dragging the child along on activities that the father enjoys but the children do not. Remember, children will do almost anything for their parents' attention, even if it means engaging in play or games they don't like.

Parent-directed "play" is really not play at all. As we've already emphasized, the ability to direct the action is fundamental to the value of play to children.

Do Some Research.

Find out about the team and/or the league and the people running it. Make sure their goals and methods jibe with your own. Be aware of attitudes or practices you may disagree with, and be ready to balance them at home.

By forcing your children to do what you want to do you not only lose many of the benefits of play, you send a message to them that their concerns are not important to you. You may also end up exposing your child to influences that are inappropriate, for example, by permitting a preschooler to watch the advertisements that accompany professional sports programs.

Competition is another issue. While it is important to teach your children about how to participate in competitive activities, it is all too easy to teach bad lessons as well. Just watch a few Little League Baseball games or Pee Wee Soccer games and you'll see plenty of parents who get overly involved, are much too competitive, and display far too much anger. Competition is good; but it can be carried too far.

Indeed, the nature of organized sports may actually make it *less* likely that children will learn positive lessons about fairness. In her book *Building Moral Intelligence*, Michele Borba writes that the increasing emphasis on competition in so many areas of our national life makes it even more vital that parents teach their children about fairness: what it is and why it's important. She opines that "the primary emphasis in organized youth sports is certainly not on inspiring fairness or good sportsmanship: it's all about winning." This may overstate the problem, but it's something worth keeping in mind.

And remember to make sure that your children get plenty of time for unstructured play. We're all aware of how much play has changed over the past thirty years. A 1998 University of Michigan study found that participation in organized sports for children aged 3 to 11 increased more than 50 percent from 1981. Correspondingly, their free play time dropped to 25 percent of their day from 40 percent in 1981. Even recess, once a sacrosanct part of the school day, is being dropped in many districts because of pressure to include more academic subject matter. Don't let this trend sentence your children to a life on the couch passing around a bag of chips.

Support the Coach.
Learn about his coaching philosophy by watching him at work. Reinforce what he's trying to teach your child, and help your child get something positive from playing for the coach.

Get Involved.
Consider coaching or assistant coaching yourself. You'll get to spend time with your child in a new setting and you'll be letting her know that you consider her participation in athletics to be an important, worthwhile activity.

Always Stay Positive.
Never publicly criticize or embarrass any child, especially your own. Help them do better by praising their physical skills, their attitude, and their sportsmanship.

Enjoy.
Keep thinking about how much fun your child is having, the exercise he's getting, and the new things he's learning. Even if he's the worst player on a last place team, your attitude can make it a winning season.

Remember that playing with your child is not something you do once and leave behind. It's a process, and it's important that you make a commitment to stay with it. Don't worry if days go by at first when you don't play with your children. Simply make an effort to pick an activity to do with your child every week. Then slowly work up to every day. By then you will have developed your own repertoire of play activities and you may never need to consult the Playactivity Chart (on the next page) again. And remember: have fun!

The Playactivity Chart

The chart that follows is intended to provide you with a quick way to come up with things you can do right now, or at a moment's notice on any day, to become a more playactive parent. Familiarize yourself with the chart now and then come back to it whenever you are stumped for things to do with your child.

AGES: INFANT TO TWO YEARS

Goals: Develop sense of self and positive relationships; explore security and permanence; stimulate curiosity.

Suggested activities: Tickle games; peekaboo; object manipulation; chase; rhythmic songs and chants.

AGES: THREE TO FIVE YEARS

Goals: Develop sense of humor; encourage testing behavioral limits and confronting fears and insecurities; teach kindness and manners.

Suggested activities: Hide-and-seek; silly jokes (for example, knock-knocks); goofy faces and voices; making an intentional mess; spinning and falling down; dancing; intentional mispronunciation and mislabeling.

AGES: SIX TO EIGHT YEARS

Goals: Exploring relationships outside the family; understanding the outside world; teaching kindness and fairness.

Suggested activities: Board and card games; silly word games; slapstick and physical humor; more sophisticated jokes and riddles; basic team activities; language games, including puns.

AGES: NINE TO ELEVEN YEARS

Goals: Cementing outside relationships; reinforcing responsibility, building confidence.

Suggested activities: Team sports and games with more complicated rules; advanced word/concept games, including logic games and Pictionary/charades.

AGES: TWELVE TO FOURTEEN YEARS

Goals: Confidence building; development of healthy self-image; strength testing.

Suggested activities: Higher-level team competition, sophisticated card games; computer games with advancing levels of play; one-on-one athletic activities.

AGES: FIFTEEN TO SEVENTEEN YEARS

Goals: Instill a passion for excellence and enjoyment in individual play; encourage an interest in lifelong play.

Suggested activities: Sports involving competition against self (running, biking, golf); complex word games; challenging games that test knowledge and analytical thinking (categories, Trivial Pursuit, chess).

3

Teaching Independence

Taking Off the Training Wheels

"My mother protected me from the world; my father threatened me with it."

—Quentin Crisp

One day Jim was sitting in his car outside Pembroke Elementary School in Birmingham, Michigan. He was curious about something his wife, Jane, said to him when he was talking to her about how fathers encourage independence in children.

"You should watch fathers and mothers drop off kids at school," Jane suggested.

"Why?" Jim asked.

"Because they have different styles of bringing children to school."

"What's *that* supposed to mean?"

"Well," Jane said, "go see for yourself."

So he did. Sitting in the school parking lot, he had a clear view of the parents who began to circle the parking lot in order to bring their children to school. For twenty minutes that first day, he simply watched how parents bring kids to school. And he noticed that Jane was right.

First, he saw mothers drive up near the school entrance in a no parking zone and park their cars. They would get out of the cars, help their children with their backpacks and then hand-in-hand walk them into the school building. A few minutes later, the mothers would emerge from the school building door, get back in their SUVs and drive off. Sometimes, he noted, the mothers would carry the backpacks or school bags into the building for their children. A few mothers carried their younger elementary children into the building. "Strange," he thought.

Then, he saw the first father drive up. He stopped his car in the same place as the mothers, leaned over and kissed his daughter good-bye. The child, who looked to be six years old, jumped out of the car and ran into the school building—never looking back.

Hmmm, Jim thought. Is this the difference? He continued to watch carefully as a steady stream of cars snaked through the oval parking lot until well after the 9:00 A.M. bell to start classes for the day. He kept a tally of how mothers and fathers did it differently. Most fathers drove their children up to the building, but few went in. Mothers, by a ratio of four to one, entered the building with their children.

Were they worried about what would happen to their children inside? Were they concerned their kids couldn't find their way to their locker or classroom? That there would be no teacher or principal inside who would help out if there was the slightest problem? Or were they just good moms who wanted to see their children in and happily ready to face the academic day?

Why didn't fathers handle things the same way?

Are fathers more callous? Less nurturing? Less protective?

Actually, the fathers he saw that first morning didn't seem less loving or concerned. Some stayed in their cars, pickups, or SUVs, watching until their children were in the building. Sometimes fathers would get out of the vehicle and help their child get their backpack on their backs. One father, dressed in Levi's and a leather jacket, jumped out of his Lexus and opened the door for his son on the other side. As the boy adjusted his backpack, the father gave him a hug and the boy walked toward the school. Other fathers also got out of the cars, but instead of walking their children into the building simply tussled their hair and said good-bye.

Half of the fathers who walked their kids into the building seemed mostly concerned about the amount of things their children were trying to carry. Apparently projects that were made at home were due in the third grade, because both fathers and mothers carried boxes for their children.

Maybe this was an anomaly and not truly representative of what happened on most mornings, Jim thought. So he spent mornings in front of other schools. He went to the upscale community of Bloomfield Hills, to solidly middle class Royal Oak, and to the bedroom community of Waterford. His observati ons were consistent. Fathers, for the most part, didn't walk their children into school. Mothers, four times as often, were more likely to walk their child into school. Dad would bring the child to school, but generally never went inside. It was "Have a good day. See you at home tonight" and then dad was gone. Moms often took the children into the building. But what happened inside? Jim was curious as to what happened when children are brought into school by their moms. And one other thing he was curious about. What happened to those kids who were dropped off at the curb by their dads? Did they have bad days, while the kids who were shepherded inside have terrific days?

What Jim soon found out was that moms didn't just bring their kids into the building. They helped them take off their coats and boots (he did his observations in the winter), hung them up for their children in the locker or in the coat room, and then engaged in a lingering farewell. Sometimes, he noted that moms would embrace their children, hanging on to them and telling them they'd miss them and that they (mom) wished they didn't have to leave. This sometimes led to children getting teary-eyed and crying.

The kids who came in when dropped at the curb? They bounced in, took off their own coats and boots, and more or less successfully got them hung up. Then they were off to talk to other children and eventually move into their classrooms. They didn't seem to be troubled or tearful about their parent not accompanying them into school. Instead, they seemed happy, playful, and ready to start their day of learning.

Jim talked to a few teachers and a principal about what he had observed.

"We try to discourage some moms from coming into the building in the morning," one principal said. "It's disruptive to the child and they seem to be creating a lot of dependency with their children."

A teacher said: "If there's any difference I've noticed it's that children who are walked in by their mothers tend to be more immature." For instance, she said she knows of a couple of children who cry when they are brought inside the building for their kindergarten class when their mother tries to leave. "These particular children are whiney during the day and ask for their mother when the slightest thing goes wrong."

What conclusions did we draw from this minor, unscientific set of social observations? That dads begin to encourage independence early on in a child's life. And that, as opposed to those parents who seemed to encourage dependence and lingering togetherness, independent children seem to deal with the social and academic activities of school in a more mature way.

Jim: I was wondering if you go out of your way as a father to encourage independence with your three children?

Kevin: I don't know if I go out of my way to try to make them independent, but I think about it a lot. Especially since we started writing this book.

Jim: I know what you mean because I look differently at what parents do with their children.

Kevin: Some parents have a need to create dependency in their children.

Jim: I agree with you. I see that in those parents whom school principals strongly discourage from walking their children into school.

Kevin: Maybe they don't feel as important in their child's life if the child isn't dependent on them.

Jim: I think that has to be a factor in many of these situations. The mothers may feel on some level that if their child doesn't need them then they are no longer important as a parent or as a person.

Kevin: I think that is sad because it hinders children. They are, in effect, giving their child the message that they are not competent unless their parent is there helping out.

Jim: I think fathers (and a good many mothers, too) value independence in their children. In our culture, independence is very important for boys and men.

Kevin: And consequently they strongly encourage it in their kids.

Jim: Don't you think that you can go too far in terms of independence, just as you can with dependency?

Kevin: Oh, definitely. There are many times when children are fearful or just need our support to get through a situation.

Jim: I agree. If we expect children to grow up too fast, then we may place unrealistic expectations on them, and that can be scary for kids, too. An overly independent child can have as many problems as an overly dependent youngster.

As we saw in Chapter 2, fathers' playactive approach translates into an exciting style of child-rearing, challenging children with new situations. As children are ready to take on new challenges, dads provide them with the confidence and independence they need to try new things. New things like going off to school on their own.

Kyle Pruett, clinical professor of psychiatry at the Yale Child Study Center, writes of behavioral research demonstrating "the tendency in men to encourage and support novelty-seeking behavior in their children is related to the father's tendency to help his offspring tolerate frustration when attempting something new." In other words, while mothers typically intervene to teach children how to complete a task, fathers prefer to hang back and permit their children to become frustrated before stepping in. Even then, fathers provide encouragement, not answers. Children thus learn how to encounter and overcome frustration in completing a task, a skill all parents can agree is fundamental to success and happiness.

All good parents understand at some level that bumps and bruises are a necessary part of learning. But mothers and fathers tend to draw the line in different places. We have all observed on the playground that when children are climbing too high or running too fast, mothers tend to step in to protect them, while fathers are more likely to resist getting involved. This often results in fathers permitting their children to take risks in the name of learning a new skill or gathering more information about their world while mothers do not. With young children this situation takes place on the playground and in the playgroup, and with bigger children it takes place in sports, with a social group, with schoolwork.

The more children act independently, the more confidence they develop in their ability to handle challenges and adapt to new situations. As children grow older and need their parents with them less and less, this self-confidence and independence translates into the ability to assess and take reasonable risks, and to think for themselves.

Paul is thirty-nine years old and has three children, boys two-and-a-half and seven and a daughter, who is four. "I do a lot of outside playing with the kids," he says, "and I notice I'm more lenient with them than my wife would be. I see that I do much less supervising and less hands-on support."

For instance, Paul says, they have a large suburban backyard which has a large play area and play equipment, such as swings and slides. "If one of the kids falls down and gets hurt," Paul reports, "I'll just say, 'You're okay. Keep on playing.'" Paul also says that he is more apt than his wife to let the youngest children swing and climb on the slide and go down by themselves. "I'm there," Paul says, "But I'm not holding their hands."

He also says that when he's working in the garage or basement with tools and one of the children wants to use a tool, he'll let them. "My wife will tell them they're too young to use a screwdriver or a hammer," Paul says, "but I'll let them—although I'll show them how to use the tool first."

When Jim's children were younger, he noticed that he would just expect them to be independent and he allowed them to take some risks. Not that he never felt fearful or anxious about the outcome. But he knew that that's how they would learn—by being independent and doing things for themselves. Two incidents come to mind that illustrate how he expected them to be independent. One occurred when his son Jason was seven years old. Jim frequently took his children to the theater for plays, modern dance performances, or musical events. During an intermission during a musical play, Jason wanted to get something to eat in the lobby. Neither Jim nor his daughter wanted to leave their seat and Jason was given the money and told to go to the lobby and get what he wanted.

"Will you come with me?" Jason asked.

"No, I think you can do this by yourself," Jim told him. Jason trudged off and was back in ten minutes with something to eat.

"Have any trouble?" Jim asked him.

"Nah," Jason replied. From that time forward, Jason knew he could handle this kind of situation all by himself.

Jim's daughter Jill, his firstborn, was always something more of a risk-taker and she often had to be reigned in. However, there were times when she needed to be encouraged to be independent and learn to take care of herself. One of those situations involved her going to rock concerts with friends. While Jim insisted on going with her for the first few times, there came a time when she needed to do this on her own. So when Jill asked to go to a concert in downtown Detroit (Jim and his family lived in a suburb), he was reluctant to let her go. But he also knew it was inevitable she would be going off with friends and for her (and his own) sake, she had to do it.

"As you know," Jim said to sixteen-year-old Jill, "I don't feel comfortable with you going off to Joe Louis Arena to a concert with your friends, but it's time you did this. I just want you to remember what I taught you about protecting yourself. You don't go off by yourself. Don't get caught in a hallway or corridor without your friends. And don't go exploring Detroit after the concert. Agreed?"

"Agreed," Jill said. As far as Jim could tell she always lived up to that agreement and she had no bad experiences in her adolescent concert-going days. But Jill did grow into an independent, competent young woman who could take care of herself in many kinds of situations.

Fathers Actively Promote Risk-Taking Behavior

Think of the ways fathers hold their babies and young children. Mothers typically hold their babies in a cuddling position bringing them close to their face. Fathers, on the other hand, often hold their babies facing outward. This may say much about the way mothers and fathers parent differently. Mothers encourage children to focus on relationships and feelings. If mothers promote a risk-taking it is often an emotional risk taking. When dads hold their babies facing away from them they may be saying, "You can face the world and conquer it." From their children's earliest days, fathers encourage physical risk taking.

As children grow up, mothers focus on safety issues for their daughters, but they tend to focus on discipline issues with their sons. Equating risky behaviors with misbehaviors, mothers may discourage sons from risk-taking behavior at the same time tolerating and expecting that they will take risks. However, trying things that are unknown and uncertain is central to gaining maturity. And as children from the first grade onward spend more time outside and away from the safety of home and family, risk-taking becomes a part of daily life.

The object is not to completely protect children from all risks, as some parents try to do. The idea in parenting a growing child is to understand that risk-taking is developmentally healthy. While it would be easy to stop children from taking risks, it would make them psychological and social cripples. This can be a source of divergence between mothers and fathers. Greg, the father of three children aged nine to thirteen, says that his wife, Pam, "is certainly more protective than I. She does recognize the children's need to grow and to become more independent, but it's difficult for her to take my lead in this area."

Often a concerted effort to change one's attitudes can do the trick. Lorie, the forty-seven-year-old mother of two teenagers, said she didn't know how dangerous snowboarding was for her fourteen-year-old son until they went into a sports store to buy some sports equipment. The clerk asked Mark if he wore a good helmet when snowboarding. Mark turned up his nose and said, "That's for nerds." The clerk didn't drop it. Addressing both Mark and Lorie, he said, "He might be a great snowboarder, but there are a lot of amateurs out there. If you collide with one of them, your brain could be scrambled—and there's no fixing that. You need to wear a helmet."

Lorie insisted Mark buy a helmet before he left the store. "I never considered making him give up snowboarding," she said. "But I could certainly monitor if he was protecting himself from getting seriously hurt." So, while understanding that the risk of snowboarding was healthy for Mark, she did begin to monitor this activity for safety.

The wise father (and mother) encourages safe and developmentally sound risk taking, while helping their children reduce the most likely sources of injury.

Risk-Taking Behavior Leads to Independence

Research has shown that fathers in general see themselves as more actively involved in encouraging behaviors such as independence. When fathers compare themselves to their wives (as Paul does), they see that they are more likely to accept and encourage more risky behaviors.

Risky behaviors, however, can take many different forms. For instance, Kyle Pruett, commenting in his book *Fatherneed* about the research he did with fathers, wrote that he found that a dad's less-immediate support in the face of frustration promotes adaptive and problem-solving competencies. Participating in a situation that leads to frustration is one form of risky behavior. When children become frustrated, they may persevere, give up, or look for help.

Risky Business

In the text we've talked about how important it is to encourage your children to take risks and act independently. We know that many of you will resist this idea because of your belief that the world is simply too dangerous to permit children very much independence. We've both heard from many parents who argue that things have changed so much since the time of our own childhoods that it would be irresponsible, even reckless, to let our children venture away from us. And we've both encountered many parents who believe that their children are in danger if they are out of sight for even a moment.

There's some validity to our instinctive understanding that the world is not as safe for children as it was at one time. Certainly a lot depends on where you live and your individual family situation. But the truth is that the world is a lot less dangerous than the media has led us to believe. For example, in *Throwaway Dads*, Ross Parke and Armin Brott devote an extensive discussion to how the figures on child abduction and child abuse have been grossly overstated for decades. Contrary to popular depictions of millions of children kidnapped from playgrounds and department stores, in fact only a few thousand (out of more than 70 million) children are abducted by strangers each year, fewer than the number of preschoolers who die annually from choking on food. The statistics for child abuse similarly overstate the actual extent of the problem.

We're not trying to minimize the risks to all of our children, nor do we wish to devalue the tragedies experienced by many families each year. Rather, we want to encourage you to make an effort to realistically evaluate the level of risk to *your* children in *your* neighborhood. All too often "better safe than sorry," a maxim that can be hard to rebut when your children's safety is involved, results in a level of overprotection that can harm our children now and in the future. In short, don't let an undefined fear of corrupt strangers behind every bush determine how you raise your children. Take sensible precautions to keep them safe, but don't be afraid to take reasonable risks as well.

Fathers, Pruett says, are not willing to rescue their children by offering relief from frustration. They're more likely to encourage them to keep trying (or, as Paul does, to "keep playing"), and that does something positive for kids: it teaches them to become adaptive, competent, and independent.

Scott, the father of three children who range in age from five to fourteen, says that he is aware that he encourages independence especially when his children are working on school assignments at home. "If one of the kids is frustrated over a task," Scott says, "I suggest they take a break and see if they can figure it out when they come back to it after calming down." Of course, he adds, he will provide help if they ask for it. "If they're trying to work it out themselves," he says, "I let them."

Mark, the father of children who are five, eleven, and fourteen, says his oldest gets frustrated with homework, too. "But he doesn't always read the entire chapter when trying to answer homework questions," Mark says. "I'll look through the chapter and when I've found the answer, I'll tell him the answer is indeed in the chapter and he should keep looking. I'll help out, but I expect my kids to put forth effort. I won't do their job for them."

Both Mark and Scott also indicate that they consciously try to let their children make as many decisions for themselves as possible. Scott is aware that he encourages independent decision-making in the areas of their choice of friends, music, food, and recreational activities, when to study, the television programs they will watch, and the elective courses they wish to take at school. "I monitor their choices, but I get involved only when they are making blatantly bad choices," Scott says.

Mark allows decision making when it relates to sports or music. "I don't care if they choose to play the drums or the violin," he says. "And it's also up to them if they want to quit hockey or soccer, or stop taking music lessons. It's their decision."

Thinking, Feeling, and Saying What's on Your Mind as a Form of Risk-Taking

Research by Jonathan Mattanah, an assistant professor at Towson University in Baltimore, indicates that in the preadolescent period, fathers' encouraging of psychological autonomy was linked with greater academic competence and the absence of both internalizing problems (such as anxiety and depression) and externalizing behaviors (such as disobedience and acting out) in their children. Psychological autonomy, as defined by Mattanah, means that children are allowed to think, feel, and say what they like without strong directives or an authoritarian approach by their fathers. Mattanah's studies suggest that when children are given the freedom to be independent they thrive and become competent in many ways. Among the ways they do well are in their academic studies as well as in their behavior. More competent and independent children, indicates Mattanah, are less likely to display behavior disorders, to be anxious worriers, or to be depressed. Mattanah also told us that both his research and the research of others show that the encouragement of autonomy by mothers and fathers promotes competence in children and adolescents.

Henry Biller, a professor of psychology at the University of Rhode Island and author of several books including *Fathers and Families,* reports that a father's encouragement of a child's independence often offsets a mother's overprotective tendencies. Excessively mothered children without men in their lives, Biller contends, are much less likely to be allowed exploratory freedom or to be encouraged to develop an assertive and independent attitude.

Not that all mothers smother their children or curtail their ability to explore and satisfy their curiosity. Katie, a thirty-four-year-old psychologist with a three-year-old son, Benjamin, is very attuned to the needs of her child to learn by exploring his environment. Chris, her attorney husband, thinks that children should be given more strict boundaries so they don't grow up to be spoiled. In many families, the opposite is true. Fathers are more willing to allow exploration; mothers may be more inclined to rein in children's exploratory desires. And, as a result, many mothers are overprotective. When Joanna takes four-year-old Emily in a store, her rule is, "We have to be within fingertip-reaching of each other." She tells Emily, a friendly and out-going little girl, that she just can't walk off on her own in a store. Joanna's husband Jamie has no such rule. "He's a lot more lenient and trusting," Joanna says about Jamie. "He's willing to let her try things."

"She's a kid," Jamie frequently comments to Joanna. "Let her try it." "We have a wooden play structure in the backyard," Jamie says. "I'll be in another part of the yard working, even though I have my eye on her. If she wants to climb it, I don't panic. But if Joanna is out there with Emily and sees her climbing it, she'll run over and put her hands under her in case she falls."

When Jim's son Jason was young he tended to wander off in stores or museums. While this was frightening to Jason's mother, Jim was much more philosophical about it: "He won't go too far and he's unlikely to get lost. He needs a chance to explore on his own." And in fact, Jason never got lost, was never kidnapped, and always sensed when he wandered too far and should come back and find his parents. That encouragement of his independence, Jim asserts, is one of the reasons Jason could go twelve hundred miles away to college at age eighteen.

How Do Good Fathers Encourage Independence and Autonomy?

As you can see by the examples used so far in this chapter, active and involved fathers protect their children from getting seriously hurt or taking too great risks. However, on the whole fathers tend to be much more comfortable than mothers with their children taking risks, exploring their environment, and trying things on their own.

Fathers encourage children to do homework by themselves and to make their own choices about how to spend their time and money and the friends they choose to play with. Involved fathers also acknowledge and listen to their children's ideas. When there's a disagreement, these fathers try to explain the rationale behind their ideas. As a result, as Erik Erickson has pointed out about psychologically independent children, they are not afraid to express viewpoints with which others may disagree.

How to Encourage Independence in Your Child

1. Be aware of your tendency to stifle independent behavior.
Many parents are tempted to intervene when things get frustrating or tough for kids. You should be aware of your need to step in and take control of a situation too quickly. There are, of course, many times when it is in your child's best interest for you to intervene and help out. For instance, if your child is getting too frustrated at trying to do homework, you may need to get involved. Or, if your child truly can't zip up her winter coat, it's time you helped out.

Yet there are many times and situations when you are more likely to create overly dependent behavior and prohibit your child from acting autonomously. Be aware of how often you carry her when she could easily walk on her own; or how often you wish to take her into school or a play group, when she really could handle this by herself; or how frequently you tell her how to do her homework when she could do it by herself with a little effort.

In other words, don't do things for your child that she can do by herself.

2. Allow your children to make their own choices.
In attempting to protect our children, we can make too many choices for them. In doing so, while we might be protecting them, we are also discouraging their independence.

Starting when your child is young, look for ways to encourage him to make his own choices. Children are quite capable of making simple decisions during the toddler years. At ages two to four, children can decide what they want to wear, eat, and play. As they get older and have better decision-making capabilities, they will be able to choose their friends, what they wish to do in their spare time, what elective classes they should take at school, how to spend their allowance, and what they will watch on television.

It doesn't mean that they have completely free choices, because parents must always play a role in monitoring their activities and setting limits. But as they show themselves more competent, then they should be allowed more free choices. Being able to make their own decisions helps them become more independent.

3. Encourage some risk-taking behavior.

We all want to protect our children from dangerous situations and serious injury. But there are times when kids will learn about independence from taking risk. It is certainly one of the great illusions for many parents that moving to the suburbs will protect children from dangers and risks. Although there may be a grain of truth in this, as we've seen, protecting children from risks can interfere with healthy development. Children need a certain amount of risk to learn to make good, sensible decisions.

If parents make all the decisions for their children, their kids don't learn to make decisions on their own. There are major differences between healthy and unhealthy risks. Going out for a soccer team, raising your hand in class to answer a question, giving a book report in front of a class, asking a girl to go to a movie with you, and filling out an application for a job, are all healthy risks that most often lead to growth and development. Unhealthy risks include fighting with another student, being sassy to a teacher, drinking alcohol, smoking, and doing tricks on a bicycle without the proper equipment.

Fathers tend to inherently recognize that risk-taking can be health-promoting. Determine whether a risk is healthy or unhealthy and teach your child how to properly assess the healthy and unhealthy aspects of risks.

4. Allow your child to express viewpoints that might disagree with your own.

It would be great if our children always agreed with us, right? Wrong. It might make life somewhat easier for parents if this were so, but what kind of children would we be raising? Children who always agree with their parents are not independent individuals. In effect, they are little more than miniature adults, automatons, or puppets. That's not really what most of us want in our children.

What parents usually want are children who are not afraid to express their own point of view. In order to bring this about, we have to encourage independent expression. Ray, the father of a nine-year-old girl, was shocked when she got so mad at him because he told her she couldn't stay overnight at the home of a new friend. "I hate you!" she screamed. "You're mean and you don't let me do anything I want!"

"Yes, I know you're angry with me right now," Ray said to his daughter. "But the answer is still no."

Ray didn't tell her she couldn't say she hated him. Nor did he scold her for saying he was mean. "Those things were not really what she felt," Ray said in relating this incident. "She was mad at me and I guess she had the right to say how she felt. I knew she'd get over it and she'd probably apologize. I'd rather have her growing up saying what she felt instead of just trying to say things that please me."

When you do disagree with your child, you can explain the rationale behind your disagreement. You don't have to tell your child he's wrong. You can say, "You're making a very good point, but I disagree with you. I know you feel you're old enough to ride your bike to the store, but you have to cross a very busy street and I don't think you're ready to take on that responsibility."

5. Listen to your child.

When you listen to your child and her ideas, you are saying that it is all right for her to be herself. When you listen to your child, you are assuring her that she is important and has valuable things to say. That brings about self-esteem. And having a solid self-esteem leads to her taking chances and being more independent.

6. If you're a father, be very involved in your child's life.

Infants who are well fathered in the first few years of life are more secure. Research shows that children who have had the benefit of a highly involved father are more curious, less hesitant, and less fearful. Other studies confirm that high involvement by fathers leads to teenagers viewing themselves as competent in academic abilities and achievements. When kids have confidence in themselves and their abilities, they are more likely to take healthy risks and act in an independent manner.

7. If you're a mother who may have a tendency to overprotect your child, then pull back.

Mothers are often fearful about taking risks. And when mothers raise children without men in their lives, they are much less likely to allow exploratory behavior. They are also less likely to encourage the development of assertive and independent attitudes. On the other hand, competent and independent children are likely to have fathers and mothers who are not only nurturing but actively promote independence. Therefore, if you're a mother and you sense you are excessively "mothering" your child, it's time to pull back. Give them a chance to explore, take some relatively safe risks, and learn to be independent of you.

4

The Magnificent Seven

Seven Tools Fathers Use to Raise Well-Behaved Children

" Without discipline, there's no life at all."

—Katharine Hepburn

We've already seen how fatherstyle parenting can lead to many positive advantages for children through play and can help foster independence in children. But it can still do a lot more. In fact, fatherstyle can help parents address the problem that concerns and frustrates them more than any other: discipline. By learning about "the magnificent seven," the techniques involved fathers use to handle discipline issues, all parents can take a giant step toward raising kids who behave while banishing family conflict forever.

The Problem

Jim has made a successful career out of helping families overcome difficult discipline problems. His thirty years of experience have taught him just how prevalent discipline problems have become. "I get questions every day, and from all over the world, I might add, from parents who are perplexed by discipline issues," Jim says. "From parents of toddlers to parents of teens, mothers and fathers have great concerns about getting their children to behave."

Not only are parents confronted by the usual gamut of backtalk, laziness, and outright defiance, but lately there has been an alarming increase in complaints about the fundamental issues of childhood: temper tantrums, meals, bedtimes, homework, and even clothing. Almost every point of contact between parents and children has become an occasion for conflict.

Consider the following three typical encounters between mothers and their children:

FIRST:

Mom: "Son, would you please clean up your room?"

Jason: "Okay, Mom, in a minute, I'm almost done with this video game."

Twenty minutes later:

Mom: "Jason, did you clean up your room yet?"

Jason: "No, Mom. But I'm almost done. I'll get to it in a minute."

Fifteen minutes later:

Mom: "Jason, have you started your room yet?"

Jason: "Nope. Soon."

Ten minutes later:

Mom: "Jason!"

Jason: "What? I said I'd get to it."

Mom: "I'm sick and tired of asking you. You'd better do it right now or I'm going to get really mad at you."

Jason: "Okay. What's the big deal?"

SECOND:

Mom: "Georgie, let's put our toys away and have some lunch."

Georgie (A toddler): "No!"

Mom: "We have toys scattered all over and we need to pick them up."

Georgie: "No! I won't!"

Mom: "Please, Georgie, Mommy's asking you nicely."

Georgie: "No! And you can't make me pick up toys."

Mom: "I'm getting upset with you and I won't ask you again. You have to pick up your toys."

Georgie: "No!" (He runs away to another part of the house)

Mom: "You'd better come back here or you'll be in big trouble."

Georgie: "No."

Mom: "Do you want a spanking?"

Georgie: "You can't catch me!"

THIRD:

Mom: "Melissa, start your homework, please."

Melissa: "I will."

Mom: "When?"

Melissa: "Soon."

Mom: "All right."

Later:

Mom: "Is your homework done?"

Melissa: "Yes."

Mom: "You did it already? That was quick."

Melissa: "Well, I didn't really do it because I figured out I don't really have to do it tonight. It isn't due until after lunch tomorrow. So I can do it in the morning."

Mom: "That sounds like you're putting it off."

Melissa: "No, I'm not. It's just that there isn't that much and I can do it in the morning."

Mom: "I'd feel better if you got it finished tonight. Then it would be done."

Melissa: "I think I should just go to bed early and then I'll be fresh and can do it in the morning."

Mom: "Now you're making excuses. Homework is important and you need to make it your first priority and get it done."

Melissa: "Geez, I wish you'd stop harping on this. You know, I think I know when homework is important and when it isn't, okay?"

Mom: "Look, there's no reason to take that tone with me. I think you'd better do your homework."

Melissa: "Just get out of my face and leave me alone, all right?"

The mothers in these exchanges were not successful in accomplishing what they wanted. The way the mothers stated their directives (as requests) is the first problem. However, we think we know what motivates moms to state their orders this way. It's because the mothers of America, having read the latest parenting books, have learned that if you love your child you will be respectful and you'll show this by asking for their cooperation, not issuing commands. The children will never question that you love them, the experts assert. After all, you're so calm, quiet, and polite, how could it be otherwise? Unfortunately, it simply doesn't work. Kids figure out that when you end a request with "okay?" or "please?" you aren't serious and you don't really plan to demand or order anything. Well, at least not until you're so frustrated that you explode in anger.

Discipline, Fatherstyle

We all know the stereotypes about fathers and discipline. Fathers are characterized as either too harsh and punitive, or else they are viewed as pushovers who are uninvolved and leave the discipline to their wife or partner. But what's the truth? Is fatherstyle discipline different from "motherstyle" discipline?

Until recently there has been no evidence regarding whether fathers discipline differently than mothers when they become full-time parents. More recent research and our own experience with dads indicate that they *do* discipline differently than moms. Mothers, say experienced, involved fathers, are often too reluctant to impose rules and are less than firm about backing them up with meaningful consequences when they are broken.

Flexible vs. Firm: What the Research Shows

Let's discuss how mothers and fathers differ when it comes to discipline. Parenting research by psychologists and sociologists demonstrates that mothers are more concerned with how the child feels than are fathers. Considerable research comparing the verbalizations of mothers and fathers has shown this as well. Fathers are more likely to use commands and repetitions while mothers are more likely to use questions and suggestions. Fathers tend to communicate less tolerance for noncompliance, whereas mothers when they use a request or suggestion are either explicitly or implicitly giving the child a choice about how to respond. A 1994 study found that mothers, because of various uses of syntax as well as in the use of semantic softeners, are significantly less directive. Mothers soften their requests in familiar ways: "If you eat your vegetables, then you'll get dessert."

Kyle Pruett has noted that behavioral scientists studying the development of self-control and conscience have long noted "differences in the way mothers and fathers try to control a child's undesirable behavior." While mothers tend to focus on the potential social and emotional costs of bad behavior, fathers go right to the consequences: punishment. For example, while a mother would scold a child who has made a crayon drawing on the living room wall by talking about how thoughtless it was and how much work it will be for her to clean it up, a father in the same situation will declare simply, "You know it's against the rules to draw on the walls. Go to your room." Other research has found that mothers apply less direct pressure than fathers in trying to elicit child compliance. In effect, fathers provide greater pressure to comply and at the same time offer a model of direction and self-assertion.

Jim and his wife, Jane, talk frequently about the discipline of fifteen-year-old Jonathan. One of the priority issues is: Why doesn't he comply with Jane's directions? "One of things we've discovered as we analyze this," Jim says, "is that Jane worries that Jonathan will be mad at her. So she doesn't get direct with him, even though she wants him to follow a command or rule."

On the other hand, when Jim wants Jonathan to do something, he doesn't care whether Jonathan is upset or not: "I just tell him what I want done. Period."

And the interesting thing is, Jonathan complies immediately when Jim tells him what to do.

This difference between Jim and Jane, and between many fathers and mothers, has important implications. Because fathers maintain an emotional distance from the misbehavior, emphasizing rules and punishment, they provide greater consistency and predictability. Significantly, they are also less susceptible to manipulation by their misbehaving children. Children learn quickly that Mom will often back off if they express contrition (sincere or otherwise), while Dad cannot be swayed even though he may demand an apology. Professor Joan Lebvre of the University of Wisconsin's Department of Family Development puts it this way: "When mothers discipline children they tend to adjust the discipline to the child's current state of mind. A father is much more likely to discipline by 'rules.' Mothers offer children flexibility and run the risk of continual bargaining." Sound familiar?

Allowing Children to Negotiate Can Be a Problem

The problem of constant negotiation over every rule and punishment is all too familiar to mothers today. Children ask their mothers to clarify their requests or commands more often than they ask their fathers. Because of the non-directive nature of their moms' requests, kids use ploys such as asking "why" so that they can delay or even avoid compliance. Consider this example:

Mother: "Jimmy, it's time to go to bed."
Jimmy: "No, it's not. It's not even dark yet."
Mother: "Yes it is. Look at the clock. It's eight-thirty."
Jimmy: "But I haven't finished playing this video game. You said I could play it."
Mother: "Yes, but it's taking too long. Now you have to go to bed."
Jimmy: "Just let me finish it. I'll be done in five minutes."
Mother: "You know you're supposed to go to bed at eight-thirty."
Jimmy: "Can I just finish the game and then I promise I'll go to bed, okay?"

Children are less likely to use these ploys with their dads. Consequently, many children, particularly between the ages of four and six, tend to ignore their mothers and obey their fathers. The definiteness of a father's commands has an effect on children that results in greater compliance. Here's an example of what we mean:

Father: "Jimmy, it's eight-thirty and time to go to bed."
Jimmy: "Okay, I'm almost finished with this game, okay?"
Father: "No, it's not okay. You shut it off and go to bed now."
Jimmy: "Can't I just finish it, I'm almost done?"
Father: "What did I just say?"
Jimmy: "Okay."

Mothers' tendency to look at misbehavior from an emotional perspective also makes them more sensitive to how they are making their children (and themselves) feel. They are thus less likely to impose discipline that might make a child cry or make themselves feel "mean." Mothers want to be liked by their children. Of course, both mothers and fathers want their children to love them, but fathers seem less concerned about being liked every day and in every situation.

The work of Deborah Tannen and Carol Gilligan confirms that women are socialized to behave in a traditionally feminine fashion throughout their lives. It is not surprising that this socialization exhibits itself when women are disciplining their children. It is also the case that women are less likely to have been subjected to strict, or even harsh discipline as children themselves, whether at home or at school. This lack of experience may contribute to their reluctance to take a firm stand with their own children.

Here's what Kevin says about his own experiences: "I've discussed this often with my wife," he says. "I attended an all-boys, Jesuit high school where the rules were very strictly enforced. Molly has expressed horror at some of the stories I've related (none of them involved any physical discipline). 'That's terrible,' she'll say. 'Weren't you humiliated?' Well, I guess so, but I viewed the discipline as a positive thing. I remember the lessons I learned, and that experience makes me more comfortable disciplining my own children."

Jim adds that he has the perspective of having raised a boy and a girl who are now adults. "I try to put Jane's raising of Jonathan into perspective," Jim says. "I know that my kids are always going to love me and be a part of the family. The particular instances of my discipline or disappointing them by holding fast to rules or angrily confronting them about their behavior has long been forgotten. What remains is this sense of being part of a family."

Guilt-inducing Discipline

There is another fundamental difference between the discipline styles of mothers and fathers. Mothers often resort to shame and disappointment when disciplining their children. "How do you think that makes me feel?" and "Haven't I done enough for you?" are common phrases mothers use in scolding their children. This is especially true as children get older and better able to feel guilt for disappointing their mothers. For example, Liz tries to induce guilt with her fifteen-year-old son by reminding him how she's done everything for him his whole life. "All I'm asking you to do," Liz will say, "is to appreciate what I've done for you your whole life. Where would you be if it wasn't for me? Your father was never around. I raised you. And now you're going to forget all that and not do what I ask you?"

Fathers, however, rarely use such an approach. Pruett writes that "[d]ads discipline less with shame and disappointment and more with real-life consequences." A visit to the playground would not be complete without at least one dad telling his child "O.K., but don't come crying to me if you fall." Or, when a teenager is spending too much time on the phone, a dad is more likely to say, "That's it. You just lost the use of the phone for the next week."

These substantial differences in discipline approaches do not affect boys and girls in the same way. It is no surprise that parents feel more confidence when they are disciplining a child of their own gender. Mothers are better at exercising their authority over daughters, as are fathers with their sons. The opposite is also true. This helps explain why so many mothers who are perfectly capable of setting limits for their daughters feel at their wits' end with their

Fathers Are from Mars

Earlier in the book we mentioned the research of Carol Gilligan and Deborah Tannen establishing that men and women have very different, but equally valid, ways of looking at the world and communicating with others. Gilligan has concluded that women are raised to sacrifice their ambition in order to make others happy, while men are expected to give up relationships to further their own achievement. Similarly, Tannen has noted that women are taught from an early age to seek consensus and ask permission, while men are raised to give orders and see that they are carried out.

All of this may be one reason that fathers are more comfortable disciplining their children, even when it leads to open conflict. In her later work, Tannen specifically studied the divergent discipline styles of mothers and fathers. In her book *I Only Say This Because I Love You*, she found that mothers experience self-doubt and humiliation when their children misbehave because they perceive it as their fault. Fathers, by contrast, do not see misbehavior as a reflection on their parenting. Instead, they see it as a failure on the part of their child.

Tannen also demonstrated that fathers get more respect from their children than do mothers. While she could not come to a definitive conclusion as to the reason, she speculated that children take their mothers for granted because they spend more time with them. Seen in this light, fathers may actually command more respect in part because their absence makes it easier for children to imagine them as threatening or intimidating.

Finally, Deborah Tannen found that fathers use harsher discipline on their sons than their daughters, even for the same offenses. While this practice fades as children grow and boys are permitted more personal freedom than girls, it supports the notion that fathers are more comfortable administering discipline because they experienced (and survived) more of it themselves.

misbehaving sons. Fathers, too, much prefer imposing punishment on their sons than their daughters.

The reasons for this phenomenon are not clear. It's possible that parents are more confident dealing with their same-gender children because they better understand how they think. We believe that many mothers have trouble controlling their sons simply because they have no way of knowing that boys often need to hear a firm and unyielding "no" before they will begin to listen. Another possible explanation is that same-gender parents can draw on the experience of their own childhoods. A good friend once told Kevin that his young sons wouldn't be allowed to get away with anything during their teenage years. "I know all the boy tricks," he said, "because I used them all on my parents."

Whatever the explanation, children can sense when a parent is uncertain and some children are ruthless in exploiting any weaknesses. Kyle Pruett explains that boys use their perception of their mothers' uncertainty and lack of familiarity with the world of boys to get away with much more than they can with their fathers. Girls do the same, finding they can slip a lot more by Dad than Mom.

It is important to note that, for the vast majority of parents, these differences in discipline techniques do not represent a conscious choice. They are simply a necessary reflection of the parents' own personalities, which are themselves inevitably shaped by gender roles. When it comes to parenting, it is undeniable that men are from Mars and women are from Venus. Consequently, many parents are unaware of the fact that they are disciplining "like a mother" or "like a father."

Fatherstyle Discipline Techniques

Our discussions with stay-at-home and single fathers as well as with involved fathers in intact families have revealed seven basic techniques these dads use to effectively discipline their children. We call them "the magnificent seven." They reflect a clearly different approach to the problem of misbehavior, and they often directly contradict the conventional wisdom among mothers and parenting experts. But experience proves that using these techniques can result in happier, better-behaved children. We will discuss each technique in turn, providing examples of how they work *better* in common, real life situations.

The Magnificent Seven

1. Don't Ask, Tell

As we noted earlier, one of the most familiar discipline problems is mothers who "tell" their children what to do by asking questions. "Put away your back-pack, O.K.?" "Clean up your toys before dinner, all right?" Asking questions instead of giving instructions is a common problem mothers share—not only with each other, but also with some dads. Books have been written about the importance of being firm, but for some parents it's very hard to learn. Women raised to be polite and to avoid conflict at almost any cost are often uncomfortable exercising authority. The difficulty with asking children to do something, of course, is that they then feel free to decline, and frequently do so.

When fathers want something done, they say it clearly and firmly: "Clean up your toys before dinner." It never occurs to most fathers to ask for assent from their children when they are delivering an order. Nor does it particularly occur to them to be uncomfortable in a role of authority. Indeed, the fathers we talked to admitted that their wives' conciliatory approach often frustrates them so much that want to scream "Don't ask. *Tell!*"

This technique is not intended to make you into a martinet or a dictator. Instead, it will help you make sure that your commands and directives are clear. Make sure it is absolutely clear what is a command and what is a request. If you don't mean it as a request (which has an option attached to it), then don't state it that way.

Make a real request like this:

"Would you like to go the movies or play tennis?"

"Would you like to wash your hair now or just before bed?"

"Could you get me a cup of tea, please?"

Al, the father of boys ages eight and ten, tends to be very direct with his boys. "I expect my boys to follow rules and live up to my expectations," Al says. "Therefore, when I want them to do something, I let them know without mincing words. The other day when we were camping and my kids were riding their bikes too close to other campers' spaces, I said, 'You guys know better. You've been camping enough to know how to respect other people's camp space. Don't ride close to anyone's tent again or you'll lose the use of your bikes.'"

Al says that he watched his kids closely for the next couple of days and that was the end of the problem.

How to use Fatherstyle to give more effective commands

The fatherstyle approach says that if you're giving an order or command, then make it clear with these kinds of phrases:

"I need you to put your bike in the garage."
"You need to take the dog for a walk now."
"I want you to take the garbage out."
"Get your pajamas on. It's time for bed."
"Dinner is on the table. Come and sit down."

Avoid using words and phrases that soften the command or directive. For instance, adding "okay" or "it would be nice if" only confuses children or gives them a way to avoid obeying the directive. What about "please"? We know that some experts advise parents not to use any words that might imply that your order is negotiable, but we disagree. Delivered in the right tone of voice (not as a question), an instruction with a "please" included can convey respect to your children and make it easier for them to comply. Not that you would accept anything less.

2. Say It Once and Mean It

In one of Kevin's dads-only panels, the conversation went like this:

David, the thirty-eight-year-old father of two boys: "One of my own pet peeves is mothers who repeat themselves endlessly, but never follow through on their threats. Not a week goes by that I fail to observe this in practice, at school, at the library, or at the grocery store. I hear mothers say, 'Stop it. Stop it. Stop it. Stop it now.' And, of course, the children *never* stop it."

Glen, the thirty-nine-year-old father of three children: "Why should they? Their mothers have taught them that they can keep on doing whatever it is they want to do without fear of any consequences."

Stephen, the twenty-nine-year-old father of a young son: "These are always the same mothers who complain, within earshot of their children, that they can't control them. They're ineffective, they know it, and they don't like it."

Jennifer has taken her three children to the library almost every week for years. It's always the same: they argue, scream, disturb the other patrons, and generally embarrass their mother. Jennifer threatens to do something if they don't behave themselves. Her favorite threat is to "leave this library right now." Jennifer's problem, of course, is that she's never actually picked up the children and left the library. Her children know the threat is empty because she has never acted on it.

Many mothers are stuck in this same rut, a variation of the endless "stop its" mentioned earlier. "They never listen!" the mothers complain. "I don't know what to do!" they cry. At this point it matters less *what* you do than *that* you do. Jennifer should have left the library the first time her children's behavior got out of control. Why didn't she? Because the prospect seemed too daunting and she didn't want to seem mean.

How to use Fatherstyle by saying it once and meaning it

Fathers take a different approach than mothers: they say it once and mean it, perhaps because they expect to be obeyed. They also speak clearly and forcefully: "Stop it!" Their children learn to listen. This method works best if you imply or threaten some adverse consequence if you are not immediately obeyed. For example, if your child is kicking the wall, you say "Stop it!" If your child does not comply, you say "Stop it or you'll go to your room." Sometimes it works even better if you announce that the punishment has already been imposed. "You just lost your TV for tonight." This is appropriate when the behavior is especially egregious or if the child is ignoring a well-established or self-evident rule (Don't Dangle the Cat Out the Window).

The key here is to mean what you say and then follow through. This is similar to an ultimatum, but not as serious. It is simply an appropriate consequence. You can't behave at the library? You won't be permitted to visit the library. You scream and cry when we visit a restaurant? No more restaurants. Simple and effective. This strategy works best if you think about it ahead of time. If your children misbehave at the library, or anywhere else, tell them before you walk in that you will leave if they act up. Don't get too comfortable yourself because, remember, you're planning to leave! As soon as they misbehave, scoop them up and go. One of the at-home dads on our panel revealed a secret: after his children kept acting up at the library he took them there *planning to leave*. He waited for the first sign of misbehavior and out they all went. That solved the immediate problem and left quite an impression on his kids, too.

3. Establish House Rules and Communicate Them Clearly

Although it isn't usually talked about as a part of discipline, there is something we like to call "background discipline." This refers to the general limits on behavior that children perceive and follow depending on where they are and who is in charge. Do your children behave the same way at the library as they do at the playground? How about when you are in charge versus when their grandparents are boss? Of course not. Contrary to conventional wisdom, especially among mothers, even the most incorrigible brats have a remarkable capacity to moderate their behavior to accord with their environment. It all depends on the background discipline.

Kevin: Recently, a woman friend of ours dropped by unannounced one afternoon to return a dish. All three of my children were at home, and she expressed surprise at the quiet environment. I even had classical music playing softly on the stereo. 'You're so lucky,' she declared. 'My house is like an asylum!' She was right; I had visited her house on several occasions. The difference between her house and mine was (and remains) background discipline.

Surprisingly, very few parents seem to be aware of the crucial role of background discipline in their homes. Only rarely do they take the time to establish house or family rules and communicate them to their children. Perhaps because they are not generally rule-oriented or because they prefer flexibility, they deal with each behavior problem independently as it arises.

How to use Fatherstyle to establish household rules

Fathers are much more likely to use "background discipline," or, in other words, establish a system of house rules. One such rule might be No Running in the House. They then tell their children about the rule (no need to explain the thinking behind it) and require them to affirm that they understand the rule. "No running in the house. Is that understood?" Not until the child says yes is activity permitted to continue. This approach has the virtue of permitting punishment to be imposed as soon as the rule is violated, without second or third chances. After all, they agreed to follow the rule.

Jim: I wanted to mention my work with juvenile delinquents in the past fifteen years. In conducting group therapy with delinquent teenagers, I've found that I don't need many rules.

Kevin: But you probably let them know what they are, right?

Jim: You bet! I go over them telling them what they are and what I expect.

Kevin: So, what happens?

Jim: Surprisingly, there are very few violations of rules. This is something that has amazed me over the years. How could I be dealing with some of the most delinquent teenagers and not have to constantly remind them of the rules?

Kevin: Because you let them know very clearly what the rules were.

Jim: Yes, exactly. And I give them a chance to ask questions and explore the consequences of rule violations if they want to do that.

Kevin: What happens if someone breaks the rule?

Jim: I simply say, "Remember what the rule is?" or "We have a rule for that." But you know, often it's one of the other kids who jumps in before I say anything and says, "You can't do that in here."

Kevin: I think the beauty of background discipline is that if you lay out your expectations early it saves a lot of unnecessary talking and reminding in the long run.

4. Demand Respect—and Get It

A lot of mothers complain that they are treated like the family maid. Or even doormats. It doesn't seem to occur to them that they are treated like that because that is how they act. It should be obvious that your children are more likely to disobey you if they have no respect for you. The fact is that an overwhelming number of the day-to-day discipline frustrations experienced by most parents stem from a failure to demand respect. Children don't listen because they don't respect their parents. They listen but ignore directives for the same reason. Many longer-term discipline problems begin this way as well. A five-year-old who feels free to leave his dirty underwear on the floor or to call you a "doodyhead" will grow up into a teenager who swears at you and proclaims that you have no right to tell him what to do.

Men demand respect because they have been raised to expect it. Paul, the father of three children, ages two, four, and six, says he regards demanding respect as an important part of raising kids. He says that if his children are disrespectful he immediately corrects them. “Even something as simple as calling me by my first name is something I’ll correct,” says Paul. He adds that he would let it slide if it was clearly meant as a joke, but if not, then he would say, “Excuse me, what do you call your father?” He says they always get the point.

When he is talking to his four–year-old son or his six-year-old daughter and trying to communicate something important, he wants respect, too. “If they don’t look at me and don’t appear to be listening,” says Paul, “I regard that as disrespect. I’ll say, ‘You need to look at me so I know that you’re listening to what I say.’”

How to use Fatherstyle to get respect

You may not want to require your children to say “Yes, Sir” and “No, Ma’am” (although it has a great ring to it), but try insisting on “Yes, Mom” and “No, Dad” instead of “yeah.” You may be surprised at how much more respect you will get the rest of the time and how many of your other discipline problems begin to disappear.

You should insist that your children demonstrate respect for you at least in the following ways:

1. Pay attention to what you’re saying
2. Listen carefully to you when you’re talking to them
3. Address you in an appropriate manner
4. Talk to you in a respectful way; use complete sentences; avoid slangy responses; talk in your presence in a different way then they would if they were with friends.

5. Refuse to Tolerate Tantrums and Other “Normal” Behavior

It has become an article of faith among parenting professionals, and consequently among modern parents, that children go through “stages” of development and that it is unwise and fruitless to stop bad behavior that is “age appropriate." In fact, the vast majority of such behavior is common only because parents don't do anything to stop it.

Kevin and his wife Molly had an interesting argument about temper tantrums long before they ever had children. Kevin saw a child having a tantrum in public while his mother watched. He told Molly that he would never tolerate such behavior. Molly informed him that the best way to handle tantrums was to ignore them and let the child get it out of his system. The two never came to an agreement on the subject. None of their three children has ever had a tantrum on Kevin's watch, but they have on Molly's. "I think the difference," Kevin says now, "is that I have made it clear that I don't tolerate certain behaviors. They seemed to catch on to this very early in life."

Rather than viewing temper tantrums and other forms of "developmentally normal" behavior as inevitable, fathers tend to see them as just another form of acting up. As such, they merit punishment, not tolerance. Fathers report much less in the way of such misbehavior as a result.

The fact is that even very young children have a much greater ability to control their own behavior than is typically acknowledged. Watch how a two-year-old behaves at his own house and then at his grandmother's. Chances are that if Grandma is very indulgent (not an uncommon situation), the youngster becomes less restrained as soon as he walks through her door. Then when he returns home, his behavior will improve again (perhaps after a short adjustment period). Offer a screaming child ice cream if he'll quiet down and see what happens. We're not advocating bribery, just making a point: children are capable of controlling themselves when they believe it is in their best interest.

Of course, at certain ages some objectionable behaviors are common (a better term than "normal," which implies that there is something wrong with children who are well-behaved) and may not warrant deploying your full discipline arsenal. Nevertheless, it is clear that the pendulum has swung too far in the direction of ignoring or indulging behavior as long as it is something a lot of other kids are doing, too. That approach to parenting is a fast way to make the least common denominator standard behavior.

How to use Fatherstyle to show you refuse to tolerate objectionable behaviors

Make it clear when an objectionable behavior occurs that you don't tolerate such behaviors. This may be done simply by saying, "We don't have temper tantrums around here" and then walking away. It's very important not to reinforce or inadvertently reward the behaviors you don't like. Often parents make the mistake of considering a behavior as common and normal and then responding to it as if it was the child's God-given right to behave that way. Don't do this and it will help to eliminate objectionable behaviors.

Fathers also usually don't hold back or hide their disapproval. Some parents may try to be tolerant and "loving" and thereby fail to show they don't like certain behaviors. If you don't approve of a behavior or action, then let your child know. You can do this with a comment, a sharply worded reprimand, a gesture, or a facial expression. But, by all means, don't hide it. If you disapprove, let it show.

6. Deploy Your Anger As a Strategic Weapon

Many mothers are scared and ashamed of anger. But anger is not all bad. After all, we all get angry, often with very good reason. Anger is only a problem when it gets out of control. Perhaps the reason mothers are wary of their anger is that they have little experience in controlling it. Mothers are more likely to go from outwardly calm to screaming when disciplining their children than are fathers. Fathers are more comfortable using a harsh tone with children and then slowly revealing more anger. This approach conveys seriousness and predictability to the children. With Mom, on the other hand, they may be able to negotiate or push the limits for a long time before she blows up. The reason? Women are usually taught from an early age that anger, and subsequent conflict, is to be avoided. And because girls are taught to value relationships, they try to use whatever methods they can to bring about compliance without endangering the relationship or getting angry.

Moreover, because they usually have little experience with managing confrontation, women often do not learn to moderate their anger. Many mothers see displays of anger, such as yelling, as a sign of their own failure to exercise judgment and control. Indeed, many women rank verbal displays of anger on a par with physical punishment in terms of their harmfulness to children. However, women have their limits, too. And when a child pushes too far while ignoring the mother's polite requests, eventually she will explode in anger or rage.

How to use Fatherstyle and anger as a strategic weapon

How do you go about deploying your anger as a strategic weapon? The most effective way is to construct mental scripts that combine your tone of voice and your language to convey an unmistakable message. These scripts should be flexible enough to fit any number of discipline situations. After all, you don't want to have to struggle to remember your "spilled juice" script when an immediate response is required for forgetting a homework assignment. Similarly, reading your "how could you be so careless" script off a note card will definitely rob it of its power!

To get started, try the following exercise: tell yourself that the next time your child ignores a directive (for instance, to feed the dog or turn off the TV), you'll reissue the command in a raised voice. If there is still no response, or if she's clearly dragging her feet about responding, you'll raise your voice to a near shout and add, "I mean now, young lady." The next step would be to punish or threaten to punish, but that's something we'll be discussing in the next section of this chapter. Used consistently and backed up with action, an angry voice and stern language will take care of many, if not most, discipline problems.

Believe it or not, this form of anger management can even work without a single word being spoken. Glen has developed a technique with his daughter that his wife calls "The Look." If she is misbehaving, he just looks at her with a deep stare, very stern. The problem stops. Many fathers (and wise mothers, too) have a "look" that stops their kids cold. It's worth developing one for your children.

Managing and deploying your anger only when necessary will also help you avoid that bane of the explosive parent, the ultimatum. Some mothers deliver a lot of ultimatums, sometimes several a day. They are almost always the result of anger, frustration, or both. As a rule, ultimatums are to be avoided. That's because you tend to deliver them when you are upset and not thinking carefully. Think of ultimatums as the atom bombs of discipline: they make an effective threat, but actually using them is a last resort.

Once delivered, however, ultimatums should be honored unless health or safety is at risk (yours or your children's). Backing down can send a strong message to your children, one that might take a long while to overcome. But take heart; sometimes things turn out for the best even when you are forced to follow through on an ultimatum delivered in anger.

Ed, the father of two boys and a girl, once got so mad at his younger son that he told him he would sit at the dinner table until he finished every piece of food on his plate. Two and a half hours later, after his brother and sister were bathed and ready for bed and he had cried several rivers, he finally complied. Ed wanted to back off, but knew that if he did he would teach his son a lesson that would come back to haunt him. Both father and son learned a lesson that day.

Remember: ultimatums are not simply statements of run-of-the mill consequences for misbehavior. If your daughter is sticking Play-Doh in the washing machine and you tell her she'd better stop or there will be no trip to the park, that's just discipline. An ultimatum is a promise of serious action, typically delivered in a much more charged atmosphere after several other warnings have been ignored.

One of the best and fastest ways to teach your children that you have limits is to "lose control" once in a while. Jim had a philosophy that he should lose it about once or twice a year with his children. "I'm a fairly controlled and restrained guy," Jim says. "Therefore, when I displayed my anger it was a big event in my kid's lives. Raising my voice, swearing, or slamming my hand down on the table was the extent of my anger, but it always proved highly effective because it was rare. Both of my children knew that when I got angry that they had clearly pushed the limits too far."

If all of this sounds as if we are encouraging you to manipulate your children by pretending to be angry, or at least angrier than you are, then you're getting the message. There's nothing wrong with using your acting skills to help your children learn how to behave themselves. By the way, there's a good chance you'll learn how to do a better job of regulating your own emotions in the process. That's something that even the best parents need to work on now and then.

7. Punish Swiftly, Surely, and Creatively

Many mothers are profoundly unsettled by the entire notion of punishment. That's why so many of them try to push off the unpleasant task on their husbands. Modern parenting magazines (which are really mothering magazines) provide some insight into just how far mothers will go to avoid punishment. They are full of articles on how to *avoid* punishing your children. One recent article on time-outs, the punishment of choice among parenting experts (if not parents) for the past twenty years, declared that the reason time-outs were not working for many parents was that they were not imposing them correctly. The point is not to punish, the article emphasized, but to teach the child consequences by removing him from your love. For this reason, the old rule of one minute for each year of the child's life is just too harsh: thirty seconds is plenty. As for scolding a child, one expert quoted in the article called it "verbal spanking" because it humiliates children. And you thought you'd heard it all!

With this kind of guidance, no wonder so many parents are bad at punishing their kids! Fathers are usually not squeamish about punishment, because as children they experienced more punishment themselves than most mothers did. They also view punishment as a natural, necessary opportunity to impart a lesson, and they know it is not the end of the world. To paraphrase a term from the education field, try thinking of your child's misbehavior as a "punishable moment" and it will help overcome your reluctance to do what needs to be done.

How to use Fatherstyle to learn to punish appropriately

The key to administering fatherstyle punishment is to do it swiftly (immediately if possible) and surely. If you observe your child kick the cat, send him to his room with an angry voice. Don't stop to ask why he did it or give him another chance. If your child calls you a bad name or talks back, send her into an immediate time out. Don't tell her how disappointed you are or how she hurt your feelings.

Jim's experience working with delinquent and troubled adolescents over much of his career has convinced him that swift and confident consequences and punishments are not only often necessary, but effective. "As a result," Jim says, "handling consequences in a matter of fact manner and also quickly often reduces future problems. And when you take the emotion out of it, even difficult teenagers accept it."

We have already seen how mothers leave themselves open to endless negotiation with their children by being too flexible. One of the cardinal errors mothers make in this regard is taking an apparently firm position that then becomes the starting point for negotiation. With this approach, "Turn your light off and go to sleep or you'll be in trouble" quickly turns into "Go to sleep soon" and even "Don't stay up too much longer." This approach to discipline and punishment is neither swift nor sure—it's a negotiation that can end up anywhere.

Remember the research demonstrating that mothers are more likely to negotiate when their children refuse to follow directions? Children pick up on this and quickly learn that with a little persistence, they can wear their mothers down. This is the origin of whining, pleading, and other obnoxious behavior. Children engage in these types of behavior for one simple reason: they work.

Parenting experts are fond of instructing parents to hold their ground rather than negotiating. That's good advice, but it doesn't go far enough. You can use fatherstyle to cut off negotiations over punishments by imposing escalating sentences. Effective fathers know that the best way to head off negotiation is not merely to stand your ground, *it's to penalize your kids for trying to negotiate in the first place*. These fathers make their initial position the *best* that their children can expect. "Turn off the TV and go to bed" becomes "you just lost your television privileges tomorrow night" and "you now have no television for the rest of the week" if the child objects or fails to comply. Children learn a very different lesson with this system: arguing, whining, and other attempts to improve their situation will actually make things worse. Not only will it make your life easier, but it will teach your children a valuable lesson about life in the bargain.

We have also found that effective fathers are also more likely than mothers to use *creative* punishments. Like many criminal court judges, they know that a punishment linked to the offense is more likely to work, especially with repeat offenders. Here's an example. Molly and Kevin were out to dinner with some close friends, fellow parents, when discussion turned to some of the frustrations of dealing with their children. Jenna, the mother, mentioned her current pet peeve: her two sons (ages eight and ten) were leaving their wet bath towels on the floor every morning. No matter what she said, they would not remember to pick them up.

Kevin couldn't believe this presented such a dilemma for Jenna, who as a very bright professional has no trouble solving much more difficult problems every day. His suggestion was to put the wet towels in the boys' beds, right on top of the sheets. His thinking was that after sleeping in a wet bed for a night or two they would remember where the wet towels go. At first Jenna thought it was inspired, but then she balked. "That's so mean!" she said. Kevin could tell she wasn't going to try it.

Don't be reluctant to stir the pot a bit. If your children aren't listening to you, whether the subject is big or small, you are perfectly justified in taking things to the next level. Often the most creative punishments are also the most memorable. That's what makes them so effective.

How to Get Started

Parents often say that the hardest part of changing their behavior is getting started. Here are a few simple and practical steps to help you begin making "the magnificent seven" part of your discipline repertoire.

Establish House Rules.

This is a necessary first step for any type of discipline makeover. It will also force you to decide which rules are important to you and which ones you can live without. Write them down if that helps and if your children are old enough to read them. Either way, have a family meeting to explain them and get your children to agree. Don't worry about setting up rewards or punishments. Those can come later—if necessary.

Get Respect.

Decide on some tangible displays of respect and let your children know that they are now expected. These may be requiring "yes, Mom," instead of "yeah" or "Pardon me?" instead of "What?" or something more substantive, such as providing complete information about school activities or cleaning up after themselves.

Monitor Your Directives.

Make sure you aren't using the "softeners" that lead to confusion. Then carefully phrase your commands in ways that are likely to lead to compliance.

5

Nurturing Emotional Intelligence

The Surprising Success of Fathers

" She runs the gamut of emotions from A to B. "

—Dorothy Parker, describing Katharine Hepburn

Seven-year-old Benjamin was watching a cartoon about dinosaurs on television with his father and older sister. A dinosaur who had been mean and aggressive to others had been in a fight and was dying. Before he expired, he said that he had seen the light and realized that for dinosaurs to survive they must be kind and work together as a family.

"See," said Benjamin, "he really is a good dinosaur in his heart and he didn't want to be mean and I think everyone else will be sad when he dies."

"That was so amazing," said Rod, his highly involved father, who spends a lot of time with both of his children. "Benjamin could understand that this character had changed and that this change would influence others. Not only that but he showed how he cared." Rod added that Benjamin's second-grade teacher frequently has reported that Benjamin is a kind and caring boy who is always concerned when another child is hurt or in distress.

Benjamin's behavior can be described as pro-social in general and empathic specifically. However, whatever it's called, the important thing is that Benjamin cares about his sister, his parents, and others. He's able—as he did with the dying dinosaur—to put himself in the shoes of others to understand and be concerned about how they feel. Feeling for others is said to be the hallmark of having empathic concerns.

What are the roots of empathy and how does it develop? Many psychologists and child development specialists have addressed this question. And the results of research and exploration have identified various factors and sources that lead children to become empathic. In a 1990 study, it was found that adults who were followed for thirty-one years and who showed higher levels of empathy were those whose fathers, like Rod, were very involved in their care. In fact, the authors of this study said it was "astonishing" to them to learn about the connection between father involvement and the development of empathic concern in their children. They also noted in their study, which appeared in the *Journal of Personality and Social Psychology,* that their findings appeared to fit with previous research that demonstrated that pro-social behaviors, such as altruism and generosity in children, were related to active involvement in child care by fathers.

When dozens of research articles on parent-child relationships are analyzed, it's found that having a loving and nurturing father is as important for a child's happiness, well-being, and social and academic success as having a loving and nurturing mother. Some studies go so far as to say that father-love is a stronger contributor to some aspects of child development. Educational psychologist Paul Amato says that a higher level of self-control in school children and higher social skills are related to an involved father. Kyle Pruett concludes that positive child care is associated with more pro-social and positive moral behavior overall in both boys and girls. Ross Parke has found that if fathers are involved in the daily care of their infants during the first eight weeks after childbirth, the babies are more socially responsive and, later, able to withstand stressful circumstances during their school years.

Other studies show that when fathers are affectionate and helpful to their children, those children are more likely to get along better with their brothers and sisters. When children have emotionally involved fathers—that is, they have fathers who acknowledge their children's emotions and help them deal with bad emotions—these children score higher on tests of emotional intelligence. Furthermore, these children tend to have better relationships with other children and behave less aggressively. Mothers, the research suggests, seem to have much less impact in this whole area of emotional regulation and peer relationships than do fathers.

So, what is the connection between active involvement by fathers and the development of what we usually call emotional intelligence these days? Don't mothers have a virtual lock on teaching children to be kind, caring, generous, and altruistic?

Research since the late 1960s seems to show that mothers may not be the prime reason children grow up to be caring and socialized. In fact, it may be the way fathers parent that leads children to grow into nice people with emotional intelligence. Like the authors of the study who thought it was amazing that fathers make such an important contribution to empathic concern for others, perhaps most of us would have to say something like, "Wow! That's interesting!" But more than interesting, this is startling and it's important for both mothers and fathers to be aware of this. However, before we try to figure out the connection between what fathers do and the development of prosocial behaviors in kids, it's necessary to consider what emotional intelligence is all about.

Emotional Intelligence

When the book *Emotional Intelligence,* written by psychologist Daniel Goleman, burst on the scene in 1995 it was a godsend for many people. Suddenly, it helped many of us understand why some children and young people were angry or couldn't resolve conflicts peacefully. Emotional intelligence soon became the newest buzzword and everybody wanted to know more about it. Why were some children seemingly born with emotional intelligence while others weren't? Was the explanation for juvenile crime contained in understanding emotional intelligence? Was it the lack of emotional intelligence? Was emotional intelligence all about brain development? Or did parenting have a lot to do with it?

Today, more than a decade later, emotional intelligence is still much discussed and studied. As it turns out, it has more staying power than many buzzwords have because it has substance. There is something vital to the concept of emotional intelligence because it is based on brain research and it takes into consideration children's learning early in life.

It will be necessary, however, to look at what emotional intelligence is, and what it isn't. Then we need to examine whether it's all based on healthy brain development and what kind of role parents play in the development of emotional intelligence. And, of course, we must determine exactly what fathers have to do with their child's emotional intelligence.

What is Emotional Intelligence?

In his book *6 Steps to an Emotionally Intelligent Teenager,* Jim defined an emotionally intelligent teenager as one who can get along with others, has the ability to monitor his or her own behavior, is able to stay calm when upset or angry, and knows how to successfully solve conflicts. In a broader sense, Goleman defined emotional intelligence by turning to the psychologists who had done the most research in the area of social and emotional intelligence. According to these researchers, emotional intelligence was composed of five main domains:

1. *Knowing one's emotions*
2. *Managing emotions*
3. *Motivating oneself*
4. *Recognizing emotions in others*
5. *Handling relationships*

These are essential traits or characteristics of children. They include the ability of children to regulate their impulses, consider the feelings of others, resolve conflicts peacefully, and keep their anger in check. And we can probably all agree that if a child can be successful in all five of these domains, we would be able to say that we had been successful in our job as parents.

It's important to point out that we knew about emotional intelligence prior to Goleman's book in 1995; we just used different names for the traits that are now understood to comprise it. For instance, many psychologists and child development experts talked about social skills. Jim, for example, has been leading adolescent therapy groups with teenagers on probation to the juvenile court since about 1992. "The focus has always been on increasing their social skills," Jim says. "Our reasoning was that delinquents acted like delinquents because they had social skill deficiencies."

Furthermore, various researchers in the social sciences were investigating different aspects of social skills. Some delved into attribution (how youth assign feelings or motives to others) and some looked at anger management while others were concerned about how kids resolved conflicts or how they became passive, assertive, or aggressive. Putting all of these threads together, those of us interested in changing the behavior of children and adolescents often conducted therapy groups with disordered youth to help them learn to manage their anger, make better choices, control their impulsivity, and use assertive, rather than aggressive, language and behaviors.

What Do Parents Have to Do With It?

Many children, if not most, who have behavior or conduct problems at home, at school, or in the community (or in all spheres of their life) may have inborn temperaments that predispose them to experiencing difficulty with becoming socially skilled. While a difficult temperament—which usually means a set of traits that make social relationships more difficult, such as impulsivity, stubbornness, short attention span, and so on—makes learning emotional intelligence harder, it is not a life sentence to social ineptitude.

However, we believe that for these children, especially, it is very important that they learn social skills and the art of emotional control early in life. As many parents and every elementary school teacher can attest, some children come to school without a clue about controlling their tempers or learning to negotiate with others. Life for these children is fraught with disappointment and failure—certainly from an emotional and behavioral standpoint, if not from an academic perspective. In elementary school, as in later school life, the two are frequently closely related.

Research shows that social adjustment is an important part of growing up. When children are not popular or accepted by their peers, they are likely to struggle in many areas of their life. But they can be taught social skills, even if they have difficult temperaments. Overcoming social skills inadquacies and becoming more socially and emotionally adept takes patience, and it takes parents who are willing to put in the time and effort to teach them how to get along with others. It also requires parents to be good, stable role models who are able to offer guidance and discipline in appropriate ways.

Many of us today are concerned about the seeming breakdown in the ability of children to reflect high emotional intelligence. More young people seem to be unable to control their anger and their tempers. Many seem to be uncaring and unconcerned for the feelings of others. And too many children and adolescents are depressed, suicidal, anxious, or unable to maintain social relationships.

The reasons for what seems to be a major breakdown in the development of emotional intelligence in a significant segment of American youth may be traced to the changes in society and the family in the past several decades. Those changes include a high divorce rate; an increasing amount of conflict between parents after a divorce; the negative influence of television, video games, and the media in general; the lack of respect for schools as a source of authority; and a decreasing amount of time that parents spend engaged in positive interactions with their children.

But parents still can wield a powerful influence in the lives of their children. And fathers have shown us one important way of doing this.

Fathers and Emotional Intelligence

As far back as 1957, three researchers first got an inkling of the importance of fathers in child rearing. In their book *Patterns of Child Rearing,* Sears, Maccoby, and Levin studied the results of a project looking at over 370 children and their mothers and made two observations concerning fathers. The first was that boys who had a warm, accepting relationship with their fathers also had a more highly developed conscience than did other boys. The second observation was that certain boys were more commonly disciplined by their fathers. "This," they wrote, "may have accounted for some of the more rapid conscience development in the boys."

More recently, other researchers have come to the same conclusion. In one research study (reported by Radke-Yarrow and Zahn-Waxler), it was found that the way parents disciplined their children determined whether they developed an empathic concern for others. Children, these experts found, were more likely to have concerns for how others felt when the discipline they received called strong attention to the distress their misbehavior caused someone else.

How Do Parents Teach Social Skills?

Lessons in empathy actually begin in infancy. How parents react to their baby's cries of distress and to their needs (like their needs for food and to have their diapers changed), are beginning to teach children about caring for others. Parents who are attentive and concerned are also teaching their children that people do (and should) care about others. We usually refer to this as responsiveness. The more responsive a parent is, the more secure a child is and the better able they are to care for others.

A second way that parents teach children to be socially skilled is by being attentive and close to a baby in a slightly different way. Children's ability to regulate their emotions has much to do not only with parents attending to a child's needs but also through a parent's interacting with their infant. That is, by looking at your baby, talking to her, playing games with her, helping her to pay attention to your gaze, and learning to take turns in conversations (albeit limited initially in infancy), you are teaching her to interact with others in appropriate ways, control her emotions, and attend to what others are saying.

Third, how you model various kinds of social skills has a sweeping impact on your child. If you are emotionally skilled and adept, your child can learn from you. Therefore, if you demonstrate emotional control, peaceful conflict resolution, empathy for others, and anger management, your child will have the advantage of a great emotional intelligence coach.

The research has been ambiguous about exactly how parents teach children emotional skills beyond these three steps. What has been clear since about the mid-1980s is that studies indicate that mothers do not play the most significant role in the development of empathy. Research, in general, is consistent in saying the following: The empathy level of children, especially boys, is significantly and positively related to their father's participation in childcare. So, this would lead us to believe that in one sense just having a father actively involved in childcare significantly increases the likelihood that the child will grow up to be more empathic.

We think it goes well beyond just being involved. Dave, a fifty-year-old father of a ten-year-old daughter, says that he wants his daughter Molly to be empathic and caring for others. And so far, she is. "She's the girl who will befriend the new kid at school," Dave says. "If another child is being picked on, Molly will stick up for them."

Dave, however, is not sure if he brought this about in Molly or not. "I am a very patient father," he says. "My wife and I are a good match. She tends to get more excited and emotional, but I'm the calm patient guy. I guess you could say that my philosophy of childrearing is walk softly and carry a big stick."

In dealing with Molly, Dave is direct, clear about his rules and expectations, and matter-of-fact in terms of how he wants things done. "I'll just say, 'This is the way I want you to treat people,'" Dave says. "For instance, I've always told her that it's more important that I hear from her teachers that she's the nicest kid in school, rather than the smartest."

How Fathers Promote Empathy

Jim: We've both looked at the research that strongly suggests that fathers play a more important role in the development of empathy than do mothers, but why do you think that is?

Kevin: I was astounded by the research, because like most everyone else I thought it was mothers who were responsible for teaching kids to be empathic and caring.

Jim: I think of mothers as being loving and teaching that you have to be aware of how other people feel. I can remember my own mother saying to me when I was a child, "How would you feel if he did that to you?" That's a pretty typical thing for parents to say to their kids when teaching them about feeling for others.

Kevin: And now we have to shift our thinking. Maybe moms said that kind of thing, but perhaps it doesn't mean as much as what dads do to impact empathy and other social skills.

Jim: But what exactly is that?

Kevin: Do you think it has to do more with discipline?

Jim: You know, I think that's what's so confusing about this finding. You would think that empathy is the direct result of a parent telling you to think of how others feel. Right?

Kevin: Yes, but that's not what the research says. In fact, studies show there isn't a good correlation between a parent's level of empathy and the child's level of empathy.

Jim: So this seems to be a much more complex transmission of a set of beliefs or values than we previously thought.

Kevin: Right. My thought is that two things happen in that transmission of social skills. One is that the father's relationship leads to identification of the child with the father and if a father shows kindness to the child and to others then the child begins to imitate the father.

Jim: Okay, I can see that. What's the second thing that happens?

Kevin: When fathers discipline they are strict about the child respecting the rights and feelings of others.

Jim: And you think that the strict setting and enforcing of rules leads indirectly to the development of empathy?

Kevin: Yes, I do. Mothers may model empathy but they may not insist on empathic behavior and furthermore they do not back up that insistence with reprimands and punishment if need be.

Jim: I sense some irony here. Moms are loving and nurturing and model empathy, but that's not enough to teach it to kids. Dads may model it, too, but they take a more strict approach to making sure children live it. In fact, dads are willing to punish to bring about empathic behaviors.

Kevin: Ironic or not, I think we both agree that dads play an important role in bringing about empathy by insisting kids live it.

Empathy, which may be said to be the basis of all social skills, may come easily and early to many children. But it doesn't to all. And that's where the fatherstyle approach comes in. Lawrence E. Shapiro, in his book *How to Raise a Child with a High EQ*, writes that when children are unkind, thoughtless, and even cruel, "Most of the time we can trace the reasons for this 'unnatural' behavior back to the home." We would concur with this.

But we would go even farther and say you can trace the reasons back to play and the relationship between dad and child. Our reasoning for this is based on research. For instance, here are important research findings:

- Studies have shown that it is an early secure attachment to father, but not to mother, that is linked with children's positive interactions with their young friends.

- Similarly, another study has found that a secure attachment to dad is linked with preschool children's cooperative and friendly behavior with peers.

The Development of Empathy

When a newborn baby hears another infant cry, that baby begins to cry as well. It's not just because the first baby was startled or disliked the noise of the wailing by a fellow infant. It's the sound of another human being in distress that triggers the baby's crying. Martin Hoffman, a New York University psychologist, believes that this reflexive kind of crying is a precursor to human empathy. Empathy is the ability to observe the sorrow or joy of another person and take it on as one's own.

According to Hoffman, empathy begins to develop in infancy and by the end of the second year toddlers are beginning to understand that everyone has their own internal feelings. Even at ages one and two, many youngsters display empathic concerns for others—their parents, for instance—and they can show helpful, comforting behaviors. By age four or five, children can understand the social situations that can cause people distress.

Some psychologists who study the development of empathy agree that there's some biological disposition toward empathy. But there are others who find in research that environment plays a significant role in shaping empathy. Parents can, they conclude, encourage empathy or discourage it.

For example, parents who show greater warmth tend to have children who have increased empathy. Also, parents who provide forceful, clear messages about the consequences for others when their children hurt others tend to have more empathic youngsters. On the other hand, children whose parents control them with anger tend to show decreases in empathy as they age.

Psychologist Janet Strayer of Simon Fraser University has indicated that every child is born with the capacity for empathy. However, she also points out that there is a lot of social scaffolding and experiences that can influence how empathy develops. This means that parents have more say than perhaps they think over how well their child develops a sense of empathy.

Martin Hoffman writes that when parents point out the harmful consequences of their children's aggressive or violent behavior, their children learn to pay attention to their empathic tendencies and to feel empathy-based guilt. Hoffman sees this as "good guilt" because children learn that they are responsible for another person's hurt.

The bottom line is that if you are a warm, caring parent, if you provide consequences when your child hurts another, if you reason with children by letting them know why they should not be aggressive or mean to other people, and if you ask your child to focus on paying attention to how they treat others, then you are more likely to raise a caring, empathic child who will treat others well.

- It's also been found that it is a father's ability as a play partner that leads to children's competence with peers.

- Children who are popular with their peers, research has discovered, generally have dads who are both more physical in play and less directive and coercive in play and other interactions with their kids.

The message of the research we've just cited is clear. Dads who engage in physical play with their children and who don't overly direct or act in a forceful way when leading play, are more than likely going to end up with a child who is popular with other kids, knows how to play in a cooperative and friendly manner, and in general just does well in social interactions with peers.

These findings tie in with the discussion in Chapter 2 about the importance of playactivity. When we described fathers' playactive style, we said that fathers are more physical and challenging in play with their kids. Now we can go beyond that and say that, yes, it is rough and tumble play and a challenging way of stimulating kids that make a difference. However, it's also the quality of *emotions* during play that makes a big difference in developing children's emotional intelligence.

When Jim played with his son, Jason, who was always big and strong for his age, things could get rough. Jason liked to wrestle and play fight. He liked to get on top of Jim when they were on the floor and thus prove he was stronger. Sometimes, though, Jason would get too rough and actually hurt his dad. "I recall," Jason says now as he remembers back to those days when they would roughhouse together, "that my dad handled it all very calmly and he never got mad. But he let me know when I hurt him or had gone too far."

As this memory of Jason's play with Jim suggests, it is the quality of emotions displayed by a dad during play that is important in helping children grow up to be empathic and socially skilled. For instance, Rod says that when he would wrestle on the floor with his children and if Benjamin or one of the girls would go too far and hurt someone else, Rod usually didn't get mad or aggressive in return. Instead, he treated it as an opportunity to remind them about the limits or about how they were getting bigger and were now capable of hurting others.

"I often turned my attention to the injured party," Rod says, "and pointed out that they got hurt and now we had to help them feel better. As part of doing that, I would say that we have to be careful that we don't hurt someone else and we have to be aware of how others are going to feel."

If Benjamin or Jason had learned through their interactions during play with their dads to settle problems in an angry or aggressive fashion, neither one of them would have become empathic and caring people. Instead, Benjamin is a boy who is popular with other kids and teachers and Jason is an adult who has become a sensitive father to his own stepson and a man who makes friends easily wherever he goes.

It's the positive interactions and the management of their own emotions in play that characterize good dads and help them teach their children how to deal with their own emotions, curb their angry and aggressive reactions, and thus learn successfully how to be a good person and a good friend.

Fathers' play style, therefore, has very important benefits for children learning to control their aggression. During play, by modeling self-regulation and by responding to their children in controlled ways, fathers teach their kids—both sons and daughters—to express their aggressive feelings in appropriate ways.

How to Use Fatherstyle to Develop Emotional Intelligence in Your Child

You can foster emotional intelligence in your child by taking some of the following steps:

1. Be a model of empathic behavior.

Children will imitate their parents when they have a solid, loving relationship with that parent. To establish a positive relationship, you must show affection, but you must also treat your child with respect and be responsive to their needs. Remember Dave, the fifty-year-old with the ten-year-old daughter Molly? He says that he is there for her, he's always calm in his parenting of her, and he respects her needs. With this kind of fathering, she is more likely to continue to love and trust him—and want to be more like him.

2. Insist on behavior that represents positive social skills and teach such skills, including conflict resolution, anger management, making good choices, and caring about others.

Lawrence Shapiro writes that "If you want your children to become more empathic, caring, and responsible, then you must expect this of them." More than just expecting it, you must *insist* on it. Require your child to be caring and responsible for how others feel.

3. Set clear and strict guidelines for treating others with respect.

Children need to know what the expectations are for their behavior. Nothing is more frustrating for children, who are struggling to please parents and control their own impulses, than to be unclear of what parents expect of them. If you are ambiguous about what you want and expect, then you can be sure your kids will be, too. Bernard, the father of three boys, points out that he is very definite and clear about what kind of behavior he wants. "I sometimes have to tell my youngest son many times about what I expect of him, but there is no doubt about what the rules are," says Bernard. (We'll talk more about the overriding importance of expectations in the next chapter.)

4. During play, use physical play and the more rough-and-tumble play of fathers.

Recall how we talked about the benefits of physical play in Chapter 2. Some of what we mentioned bears repeating in the context of emotional intelligence. The playactive style helps to stimulate children in positive ways, and it also provides opportunity for the competition that many children (especially boys) need. Moreover, physical play offers the opportunity for you to control your emotions and deal with the almost inevitable "too rough" play that results with calmness, caring, and limit-setting that is essential for children during the toddler and preschool years when they are learning to master their emotions and learn the rules of social interaction.

5. Be willing to back up your guidelines with reprimands or punishment. Good fathers are not only very clear about their expectations; they are also willing to back up their rules and limits with punishment. They don't feel as emotional or as conflicted about reprimands and punishments as mothers often do. You can learn from good fathers by being willing to enforce your rules, expectations, and limits with effective and appropriate punishments.

6

Expecting the Best

How to Create a Culture of Expectation in Your Home

“ Life is largely a matter of expectation. ”

—Horace

In the last five chapters we’ve discussed many of the things all mothers and fathers can do to improve their parenting using the elements of fatherstyle. As we noted in the Introduction, each successive chapter of the book has greater relevance for your growing children. The power of play, teaching independence, and adopting a new system of discipline are all vital to enjoying the benefits of fatherstyle. Once your children reach a certain age, however, you will find that you can have the greatest influence on your children’s success and happiness by challenging them to do their very best. That’s what this chapter is all about.

As your children grow there are fewer opportunities to spend large blocks of time with them playing, talking, or disciplining. At the same time, your growing children are experiencing more challenges and more opportunities to make their own decisions. This is when it becomes essential to create a home environment that provides them with the support and motivation they need to succeed.

One of the most important ways fathers parent differently from mothers is by expecting excellence from their children. Indeed, Kyle Pruett has referred to the expectation of achievement as "classically more related to father care than to mother care." As we have already seen, from play through discipline to school work, fathers consistently challenge their children more than mothers. We'll now take that notion a step further, demonstrating how involved fathers use "expectation parenting" to help their children become happy, achievement-oriented adults who demand the best from themselves. Then we'll demonstrate how you can use this expectation parenting approach to help your growing children throughout their lives.

The Meaning of Expectation

Before we go any further we should take a moment to define what we mean when we refer to expectation. Dictionaries define expectation as an assumption, hope, or supposition that something, usually positive, will happen. The notion of anticipation and looking forward to something is an essential part of expectation. Significantly, expectation does not imply certainty. Just the opposite, in fact: uncertainty is inherent in the concept.

Kevin: Some people expect their child to realize a very specific outcome. For example, "My daughter will grow up to become the first woman President of the United States."

Jim: Those kinds of expectations are rarely fulfilled, and they can be a lot more harmful than helpful. When we refer to expectations for children, we mean simply hoping and anticipating that they will behave in a certain way.

Kevin: In other words, expectations in reference to people make sense only when they focus on behavior, character, and effort, not outcomes.

Jim: Right. But parents naturally have expectations regarding outcomes. For example, what kind of adults their children will become.

Kevin: Absolutely. We'll talk about those kinds of expectations a little later, but for the most part we'll be talking about expectations regarding effort and character.

Having expectations regarding effort means requiring your child to demonstrate determination and hard work in pursuing her goals. Having expectations regarding character means requiring your child to demonstrate honesty and kindness, among many other qualities. It's very important that you keep this distinction in mind as we proceed to talk about the importance of expectations and how to formulate and communicate them to your children.

The Importance of Expectations

We all know that expectations can play a powerful role in happiness and success. Not only our own expectations, but the expectations of others who we admire, respect, and love. Many of us are more motivated to fulfill the expectations others have for us than we are our own expectations for ourselves.

What is true for adults is more true for children. In *Raising Motivated Kids,* award-winning parenting author Cheri Fuller writes that "[k]ids who succeed and overcome obstacles in school and life usually have one experience in common: They have at least one person in their life who had high expectations for them and provided support and structure for their dreams." She notes that "kids are particularly attuned to the expectations of their parents and teachers, and they tend to fulfill them." Psychologist Carol Kelly agrees: "[w]e know from numerous studies that children usually remain loyal to parental expectations." A famous study has shown that children respond to high expectations in the classroom, too—performing to the level of their teachers' expectations regardless of their innate abilities. Dr. William Sears believes strongly in the importance of expectations: "Children very often live up—or live down—to their parents' expectations. Praise a child for being kind and she will look for more opportunities to show kindness. Tell her she's not very good at softball and she'll probably start dropping easy fly balls. Children know what their parents expect from them, even when the expecta-

Expectations and Gender

In Chapter 4 we discussed the effect of gender on discipline styles. It is a sad fact that, notwithstanding tremendous strides over the past decades, society is still dominated by stereotypes based on gender. Many authors have documented how children are still raised to believe that parenting is a woman's job and how such stereotypes can prevent them from becoming happy, fulfilled parents. Such stereotypes, which are inextricably intertwined with gender-based expectations, can be harmful to our children.

Kevin: In the fall of 2004 I had the pleasure of attending an event put on by a local parenting education group. The featured speaker was Michael Gurian, author of The Wonder of Boys *and a well-known proponent of the notion that the brains of boys and girls are so biologically different they should be treated and educated differently. Mr. Gurian was informative and entertaining, and he clearly impressed the standing-room-only audience of mostly mothers. But while his message contained some thought-provoking elements, his overemphasis on gender drew attention away from some fundamental truths about our children and our responsibilities as parents.*

It's always tempting to seize upon a simple approach—backed up by science, no less—to guide our parenting. This is especially true for fathers, who typically spend less time with their children than do mothers and are often on the lookout for shortcuts to better parenting. But despite Mr. Gurian's view that children's gender is one of the paramount factors in understanding their behavior, it is so far from the whole story that relying upon it to guide our parenting would be a grave error.

For example, gender tells us next to nothing about an individual child, especially our own children (whom we presumably already know very well). As Susan Gilbert, author of *A Field Guide to Boys and Girls*, writes, "[g]ender research is about groups of boys and girls, not individuals." Indeed, most children fall outside of stereotypical male or female behavior. "When it comes to gender-typed behavior, most children don't fit the mold. Even when researchers find differences between boys and girls, the differences are fairly minor, and it's often fewer than half the children who skew the results," Ms. Gilbert notes. In short, gender by itself means very little for parents who have all kinds of experience and other information about their children as individuals.

Moreover, gender does not even tell us as much about individual children as any number of other personality traits. Mr. Gurian himself acknowledges in his talk that "gender is only one difference among many." And these many other differences are actually *more* important than gender when it comes to children's behavior. Susan Gilbert emphasizes that "[w]e're bound to see more variation between any two children, regardless of their sex, than we'll see between a group of boys and a group of girls." This is difficult to remember when we see behavior that confirms our view of the typical boy or girl, but it is worth remembering if we hope to understand and affect our children's behavior.

Finally, there is a real potential for us to cause harm to our children by relating to them based primarily on gender expectations that may very well not apply to them. Boys who are not focused on competition or sports may develop feelings of inferiority if their parents nevertheless insist on treating them like "most boys." Similarly, girls who are not as interested in peer relationships or the latest fashions may feel abandoned by parents who are not interested in recognizing their other strengths. It would be a shame if we stifled our children's unique qualities and interests because of an overreliance on their gender to guide us.

Our gender-based expectations can too easily become straitjackets discouraging our children from exploring their own unique natures and personalities. This is not to say that Mr. Gurian's view is without some merit. Most girls *are* different from most boys, and understanding that fact can undoubtedly help teachers, coaches, and other adults who deal with large groups of children do their jobs better. We cannot expect professionals to get to know each child well enough to determine the ways in which they may depart from stereotypes of male and female behavior.

But there are no shortcuts when it comes to parenting. Despite the attraction of any number of so-called scientific approaches to child rearing, we can be good parents only by taking the time to get to know our children. First and foremost, that means realizing that there is a lot more to them than whether they happen to be boys or girls. Everyone would be better off if we thought less about gender and more about the countless other characteristics that go into making our children the endlessly surprising individuals we are lucky enough to know. Certainly they have a right to expect no less.

How do you go about raising children who are free from gender stereotypes? The best way is by example: demonstrate the fallacy of the notion of "men's work" and "women's work" in the way you live every day. Such teaching by example can be quite powerful. Research conducted by Kyle Pruett of Yale University has found that stay-at-home fathers raise children who are much more comfortable behaving in ways at odds with traditional gender roles. For example, preschool boys with full-time fathers are just as comfortable playing with girls in the doll corner as they are interacting with their fellow boys at the car and truck shelf. These children, Pruett found, are also more likely to have friends of the opposite sex as they grow into adolescence. "As a group," Pruett has noted, "they tend to be more in touch with who they are . . . [with the] self-assurance of being accepted for who they really are." They maintain these attitudes well into adulthood, remaining more supportive of workplace equality and non-traditional family arrangements than the general population.

Mr. Gurian says that "human biology is primal, and we neglect it at our peril." Point well taken. But while biology is important, it is not destiny. And neither is gender.

tions have gone unsaid. Parents' expectations become part of children's beliefs about themselves."

We all know this, almost instinctively. After all, we were all children once, and many of us still have parents with expectations. We can remember how much it meant to us to know that our parents expected us to do a certain thing or act a certain way.

Having high expectations for your children helps them believe that they are capable, talented, and likable. Parents' expectations are a very powerful motivator for children. Let your children know that you expect them to do their best.

The Danger of Low Expectations

During the 2000 presidential campaign both the Democratic and Republican nominees argued over whether low expectations—of parents, schools, and society in general—were a factor in making it harder for minority children to succeed in school. We're not sure they ever agreed, but they were definitely on to something. As we've just seen, high expectations can be a powerful motivator for children to succeed and be happy in whatever pursuit they choose. Conversely, low expectations can dull ambition and so cripple self-confidence that children actually perform worse than they would in the absence of any expectations at all.

Lately it has become fashionable to discourage parents from expecting "too much," perhaps out of a fear that unreasonable expectations will actually make it more likely for children to fail, or to achieve their goals at too high an emotional cost. There has certainly been a backlash against the so-called "over-scheduled child" and his or her companion, the pushy parent. Some of this is entirely warranted. At least where our children are concerned, however, the danger of expecting too little far outweighs the potential drawbacks of expecting too much.

Recall the research we mentioned earlier: just as children will live *up* to their parents' high expectations, children will live *down* to their parents low expectations. It is thus vital that we learn to set appropriate expectations for each of our children.

Kevin: One of my biggest pet peeves is when people observe a misbehaving child and comment "he's just being three" or "it's just the terrible twos." Just as high expectations can result in good behavior, low expectations can cause (or reinforce) bad behavior. It's no accident that, for adults, deciding that poor behavior is somehow "natural" lets them off the hook. They don't have to get out of their chair to do anything about it. It's the worst form of parental laziness.

Just as many parents who are poor disciplinarians are undisciplined in their own lives, parents who are reluctant to set high expectations for their children often have low expectations for themselves. If this describes you, it is essential that you prevent your own issues from limiting your children's potential. Fear of failure is perfectly natural, but too much fear guarantees failure.

Taking the time to create appropriate expectations for our children is a difficult and time-consuming process. And, like painting the Golden Gate Bridge, the job never ends. Having no expectations is worse than having low expectations. At least the children of parents with low expectations know that they cared enough to think about the subject.

Expecting Fathers

We've all heard of expectant fathers, but what about *expecting* fathers? In Chapter 3 we explained how involved fathers encourage independence in their children by permitting them more freedom to explore the world and make mistakes. Closely related is the father's tendency to expect his offspring to tolerate frustration when attempting something new. This expectation has been shown to be particularly strong in the case of older children and daughters, who will often cite it as a crucial element in their upbringing.

Citing differences in parental behavior when helping children master a difficult task, Kyle Pruett writes:

Showing a strong educational motivation in their approach, mothers will more typically nudge the ring into the child's reach or start writing part of the letter before the child reaches a frustration level that might interfere with the ability to complete the task. Fathers in the same scenario, on the other hand, tend to hang back a bit longer, encouraging the child, verbally or with their physical presence alone, to bear the frustration and stick with the task, thus often enabling the child to pass the point at which help might have been offered by the mother.

Pruett notes that when the latter approach works, the feeling of mastery can be pretty gratifying for both the father and the child, and the experience is an interesting complement to what might be felt when the mother assists the child.

Many of us have observed this phenomenon. Most mothers don't like to see their children struggle, become frustrated or, heaven forbid, cry. As their children grow, their priority tends to be making the child "feel good about himself" rather than making sure that he learns what he needs to know. Just as we observed in Chapter 4 with regard to discipline, mothers are more process oriented, fathers more concerned with outcomes.

Dave, one of the fathers we met in earlier chapters, finds that he often expects more from his daughter Molly than does his wife. "I sometimes have higher expectations for Molly in physical events. I push her to do her best in athletic events such as swimming, whereas my wife is more of a 'I just want her to have fun' kind of person. I also want her to have fun first and foremost, but sometimes life requires extra effort to be successful, and I encourage her to really try her hardest. I love the expression on her face when she does something she originally did not think she could do."

Greg, another father we met in earlier chapters, agreed that he is the one who expects the most from his children. "I notice that I tend to keep the standards high for my children. There is definitely a push for them to achieve." He used a memorable phrase to describe his approach: "I am the bar-raiser in my family (at least more so than my wife). My challenge is to raise the bar without lowering the boom."

Becoming an Expectation Parent

Now that we have some understanding of the overwhelming power of parental expectations, let's discuss how you can make expectation parenting work for you and your children. There are three steps to becoming an expectation parent: formulating expectations; communicating them to your children; and putting your expectations into practice.

Formulating Expectations

Your first step is to formulate your expectations. This is more difficult than it sounds. You don't have to sit down with your spouse and make a list as soon as you learn that you'll be having a child, but you will have to give your expectations serious thought. Many expectations are a given: politeness, kindness, responsibility. Our parents expected these qualities, and society as a whole does, too. These expectations probably don't require much thought for most families.

The hard part, of course, comes in deciding what constitutes something like politeness. A quick glance at Judith Martin's "Miss Manners" newspaper column will demonstrate that many parents are uncertain about what it means for a child to be polite. Must they introduce themselves to new people? Do they have to send a thank-you note for a present they unwrapped in front of the giver? Do they have to ask to be excused from the table? These points might sound picky, but taken together they are what makes one household different from another.

This example also illustrates something else about expectations: some are very important, others less so. Your expectation that your children go to school every day without getting suspended or expelled counts as very important. Your expectation that your child remember to place his dishes on the counter near the sink after finishing a meal is not so important (though it may seem critical when you have to remind him for the four hundredth time).

Make sure that your expectations are well thought out. This should go without saying, but many of us are guilty of hastily turning something into an expectation and then regretting it later. Why are you forcing your child to participate in band at school if he hates it and you don't have a sound reason for requiring it? Likewise, don't insist on some behavior just because everyone else does. You may have a pleasant mental picture of the whole family attending church together every week, but if you're not that religious and it causes conflict, what's the point? By the same token, of course, don't abandon an expectation merely because you find yourself in the minority of parents.

Once you have given some thought to your expectations, you should discuss them with your spouse out of your children's hearing. Most likely you will agree on most things, but don't be surprised if you differ from time to time.

Kevin: I'm a neat freak, not to mention obsessively prompt, so I consider it a very important matter to be neat and timely. My wife is less concerned on both scores. So we discuss things and compromise.

One useful way to start a discussion with your spouse is to talk about who feels more strongly about a particular issue. Perhaps that person can set the expectation, anticipating that the other spouse will get a turn on something she feels more strongly about later. (In Chapter 7, we'll discuss in some detail how to become a parenting team.)

After a while you'll have a set of expectations that reflect your view of the world and the things you hope to teach your children. But you're only getting started. You still face two considerable challenges: communicating your expectations to your children, and putting your expectations into practice.

Communicating Your Expectations

Once you have formulated reasonable expectations, your second step is to communicate them to your children with clarity. This means using what we call "terms of expectation" (like terms of endearment, only more focused!): "I expect you to . . . ," "We expect that . . . ," "I don't ever expect to hear . . . ," and so on. Don't speak in code. Many parents complain that their children don't listen, but we find that a lot of those parents are not saying what they mean. Use terms of expectation all the time, and also make it clear that failure to meet expectations will have consequences.

Jim: Many parents use "parentese," a kind of code language that rarely works very well with children. Parents need to spell things out so there can be no misunderstanding the message or its importance.

Kevin: It reminds me how I have to remind my wife not to use "doctorese" when she's talking about illnesses. She'll say that someone is "very uncomfortable," which really means that they're in excruciating pain, or she'll say that someone's "condition is worsening," which means that they won't be around next week. It's hard to follow.

Jim: It's similar with kids. They're not mind readers, after all.

With younger children, of course, clearly communicating your expectations will present a greater challenge. For one thing, they may not even be capable of understanding the word "expectation." They may also become frustrated almost before they get started. Your best bet with very young children is to use terms of expectation with an explanation that fits their age. For example, with a three-year-old you might say, "Daddy and I expect you to put your dirty clothes in the hamper. That means it's your job to make sure your dirty clothes are in the hamper before you get into bed. If you don't remember to do your job every night, daddy and I will be very disappointed and you won't be allowed to watch *Blue's Clues* the next day." That statement contains all the necessary elements: terms of expectation, a restatement in age-appropriate words, and a negative consequence that will register with the child.

By the way, the negative consequence can be anything that will make an impression. Taking away a cherished privilege for one or two days is simple but effective. And there should be positive consequences, too. If your child does a great job on a particularly challenging expectation, let him know it. A little later we'll talk in more detail about the importance of praising our children when they succeed.

In the next section on putting your expectations into practice we'll talk about how you can remind your children of your expectations once you have communicated them.

Putting Your Expectations into Practice

Now that we've discussed the importance of high expectations and you understand the process of formulating expectations and communicating them to your children, we'll describe how to put your expectations into practice every day.

While we've already talked about how to communicate your expectations, there's still the matter of letting your children know that you're embarking on a program of expectation parenting. We think you should make an announcement of some sort. If you're starting from scratch, a family meeting where you lay out the new system is only fair. If you're merely tweaking your own system, a brief mention over dinner will suffice.

Like adults, children will forget what they've been told if they're not reminded. We suggest making a list of expectations for each child. Make several copies if necessary, one for the mirror in their bedroom, one for their bulletin board in the kitchen, one for their backpack, one for their locker at school. For younger children, you may want to post a list (in pictures if necessary) at the top of the stairs or at the back door.

Kevin: I know one mother who made a poster that went at the top of her stairs. It reminded her preschooler to get dressed, put her dirty clothes in the hamper, go to the bathroom, and brush her teeth before coming down to breakfast. Simple and effective.

A laminated index card in a first grader's backpack is similarly creative. Remind your children to check their lists every morning for a week. After that, they're on their own.

The next step is to monitor your children's performance. This is a lot of work, but it will become less burdensome as your children improve and, in any event, you'll get used to it. Watch and see whether Carol remembers to take her completed homework to school. See if Donnie brings all of his cold-weather accessories home at the end of the day. Are rooms getting cleaned, dishes cleared at the end of the meal, thank-you notes written? The list goes on and on, and during this period you have to be on top of it all.

Dealing With Failure

How do you handle your child's failure to meet an expectation? Do nothing the first time you see a failure. Not only should you remain silent (other than reminding your children to check their lists every morning), you should not intervene in any way. *Don't do it yourself.* This is next to impossible for many parents (especially mothers), but it is absolutely vital.

After the second time you see your child fail an expectation, take her aside and remind her of the expectation, how you carefully communicated it, and the consequences of failure. Briefly ask why she failed to meet the expectation in an age-appropriate way: "Why can't you remember to make your bed in the morning?" Then provide her with an opportunity to fix the situation (for example, put away the folded laundry that's been sitting on the floor of her room for two days) and impose the consequences that you have determined are appropriate. The third time it happens, add another step to your response: suggest a solution that will head off failure the next time. For a simple example, if your son is constantly late for his safety patrol post in the morning, suggest that he get up earlier. Go through this same exercise for as many times as it takes.

It's all well and good to talk about cleaning up a bedroom, but what about something like completing homework that's difficult? Here's where you're most likely to encounter the frustrated child. In this instance you can follow the steps we have already laid out, with an additional element: motivation.

For example, if your son is struggling to write all of the lower case letters, and you've already suggested one or two things that might make it easier (for example, tracing the letters first), you offer a break to do something he enjoys with the understanding that at a certain time you will return to finish the work. ("We'll play one game of Go Fish after the next group of letters, then you'll come back and finish the assignment.") Use this type of motivation sparingly, of course, or your child will catch on and demand it as part of every task he's expected to complete.

What if he starts to whine or cry? (*Kevin: Believe me, I've been there.*) Soothe him with words and physical contact, offer words of encouragement, but don't do it for him. You may find that a one-page assignment will take an hour, but your child will emerge with an invaluable sense of accomplishment.

Keep to this plan of putting your expectations into practice and you will see results very soon. Don't give up if things get rough, just follow the plan. Adjust your approach to account for different tasks, different expectations, and differences among your children. If you need to go back to start with one of your children on one or more expectations, then do it. Just think, by hanging in there you'll be teaching your children an important lesson in overcoming frustration! (And you may even learn the same lesson yourself.)

Dealing With Success

Many parents forget to do something when their children meet their expectations. After all, they only did what was expected, right? Wrong. *Always remember to praise your children when they meet your expectations, or in some cases when they come very close.* In the example above of the boy struggling with his homework, the most important part of the whole exercise is praising him at the end. If he makes a great effort and the result is only so-so, use your judgment. Is this his best work? If so, praise him loud and long. If not, don't offer false praise. Better to tell him "I know you can do better than this," and try again.

Whatever you do, always keep things positive. Never use expectations to demean, humiliate, or scare your child. Some parents find it helpful to keep some kind of record of their children's successes. Be creative! Remember the gold star charts many of us had in grade school? You can make one of your own to record your child's progress. This technique may be especially effective when your child is tackling a task that has many steps or presents a special challenge. For everyday successes a dessert or some special parent-child time reading or playing ball is an excellent reward. Don't go overboard, and whatever you do, don't reward your children with money or anything other than token presents. You'll be sending a message (and setting a precedent) you'll come to sorely regret later.

The Five Arenas of Expectation

Remember: fatherstyle expectation means setting high standards that challenge children to the point of frustration and then helping them achieve mastery despite their frustration. We've developed five "arenas of expectation": the five main areas in which parents can develop expectations for their children, arranged roughly in ascending order of age and importance:

1. *behavior*
2. *character*
3. *academics*
4. *athletics and other activities*
5. *adulthood*

We will talk about each of the five arenas of expectation in turn, describing what expectations are reasonable, how parents can go about establishing expectations, and how they can handle problems that will inevitably develop.

Expectations Regarding Effort and Behavior

In Chapter 4 we saw how important it is to establish rules and enforce them consistently. But discipline, which is another word for behavior control, does not end once your children learn to put away their toys and to chew with their mouths closed. As children grow, they (we hope) no longer have to be reminded about such basic things. But that doesn't mean that their behavior ceases to be an issue. Instead, it means that the type of behavior that concerns parents changes, as do the means parents use to prevent or control it. For older children, social behavior (how they interact with their peers and adults) and potentially self-destructive behavior (substance abuse and sexual relations) come to the fore.

Many parents believe that their expectations regarding their older children's behavior have little or no effect. In fact, several years ago a best-selling book asserted that children's friends have a greater influence over their behavior than their parents. While much of the research behind that conclusion has

Just Say Dads

For teenagers, demonstrating character often means making decisions about whether to engage in dangerous behavior because "everyone else is doing it." Fathers can play an important role in helping their adolescent children resist peer pressure and make healthy choices. For example, according to recent studies, fathers play a major role in whether or not their children choose to abuse alcohol and drugs. A national survey by the National Center on Addiction and Substance Abuse at Columbia University (CASA) found that teens in two-parent families who have fair to poor relationships with their fathers are 68 percent more likely to smoke, drink, and use drugs. By comparison, teens raised by single mothers alone were only 30 percent more likely to smoke, drink, and use drugs.

"Fathers play a pivotal role in turning their kids off illegal drugs, alcohol and tobacco," says former White House Drug Policy Director Barry McCaffrey. "Fathers need to be straightforward and understand that what they say to their children matters deeply and will have a lifelong impact." In a 1998 national study conducted by the Kaiser Family Foundation and Children Now, youths aged ten to fifteen reported that their fathers were good, credible sources of information on difficult issues such as AIDS, sex, drugs, and alcohol.

But most fathers do not take an active role in discussing substance abuse with their children. Survey data from the Partnership for a Drug-Free America reports that fathers talk less often with their children about the issue of drugs than do mothers. Only 39 percent of fathers have talked to their kids "four or

since been debunked, it reinforced a common feeling that children care less about what their parents think as they near adulthood. That is a dangerous myth. Actually, children care more about what their parents think as they begin to confront more adult decisions.

Expectations Regarding Character

Character is the older sibling of behavior. We describe a preschooler as well-behaved, but we talk about teenagers as having good character. What do we mean when we talk about character? Broadly stated, it refers to an individ-

more times" in the past year about drugs, compared to 48 percent of mothers.

One of the reasons fathers do not talk more with their children about substance abuse is their own underestimation of its dangers. The CASA survey data found fathers were less likely to understand the negative consequences of drug use. Fathers are also less likely to use "parenting skills" such as monitoring their child's activities, making and enforcing rules, and asking about their child's day and their close friends.

It's up to all fathers to change this situation. Tom Hedrick, director and founding member of Partnership for a Drug-Free America, agrees. "Those of us who are fathers have to step up to the plate and start talking to our kids about the real dangers of drug use and other risky behaviors. Not enough young people are getting a clear message about substance abuse, and research shows parents talking to kids early and often can make all the difference. We simply can't rely on mothers to do all of the heavy lifting." Joseph Califano, Jr., of CASA at Columbia University, declares that "the statistics should be a wake-up call for dads across America to become more engaged with their children."

The time is long past due for fathers to assume more responsibility for helping our children avoid substance abuse. We must all make a firm commitment to learn about the dangers drugs and alcohol pose to our children and to talk to them early and often about this subject. Let's all let our children know that everybody *isn't* doing it.

ual's moral constitution, the sum of his habits vis-à-vis the rest of the world. Character is not something we're born with, though our innate qualities can affect it. Character is something we all learn as children. Kevin Ryan and Karen E. Bohlin of the Center for the Advancement of Ethics and Character at Boston University have written that "[b]ecoming a person of character . . . means gaining control of one's own clamoring desires, developing a deep regard for others, and being ready to put aside one's own interests and sometimes even one's needs in order to serve others."

This is plainly not something children can achieve on their own. It may take a village to raise a child, and character education in schools may be the latest rage, but parents have the primary responsibility for developing character in their children. Ryan and Bohlin set out five principles parents can follow to help develop good character in their children: (1) make parenting your priority, (2) don't be afraid to exercise your authority, (3) create a community of good examples, (4) consciously build your family, and (5) become involved in your children's school life.

These principles make good sense. But we think you can be most effective in helping your children develop character by focusing on expectations. Let your children know about the features of a good character. Many families do this through their religion, but you don't have to be religious to teach character. Your example is important, but you must also expect your children to have good character. Expect them to have and show respect for others.

Expectations Regarding Academic Performance

Academic performance means a great deal in America today. No longer can a young person without a college degree expect to earn enough money to support a family. Even a college degree is only one step on the way to most careers. Even if your child ultimately decides to become a garbage collector or (egads!) a writer, she'll need a solid education. And the more education, the more options she'll have. It's all about choices.

In their book *Spark Your Child's Success in Math and Science,* Jacqueline Barber, Nicole Parizeau, and Lincoln Bergman provide sound advice: "Have and convey the highest expectations for your child's academic success. If the message your child gets—because you're afraid to aim 'too high,' or you sense her reluctance—is that it's okay to do okay, what more should she expect of herself than 'okay'?"

Involved fathers know that they can have a tremendous, positive effect on their children's academic performance. Of course, research has long confirmed that parental involvement is a crucial indicator of children's success in school. It is well established that parental involvement benefits students by helping them to achieve higher grades, better attitudes toward school, better attendance, higher rates of homework completion and graduation, and greater enrollment in college.

The 1996 National Household Education Survey produced the first national data on the effect of fathers' involvement at school. Researchers concluded that both resident and non-resident fathers who were involved in their children's schools provided significant, and often startling, educational advantages to their children *that were not realized when only their mothers participated in school activities.* These benefits were found to be the most significant for students in grades six through twelve.

Comparing the involvement of parents with student academic achievement and behavior, the researchers specifically found that:

1. *Students in traditional two-parent families were 43 percent more likely to receive primarily "A" grades if their fathers were "highly involved" in their schools;*

2. *Students in middle and high school whose fathers did not live at home were also 43 percent more likely to receive primarily "A" grades if their fathers participated in even one activity at school;*

3. *Children of "highly involved" resident fathers were 55 percent more likely to enjoy school than children with "uninvolved" fathers;*

4. *Children of "moderately involved" non-resident fathers were also more likely to enjoy school than children with "uninvolved" non-resident fathers;*

5. *Students in middle and high school were 88 percent more likely to participate in extracurricular activities if their resident fathers were "highly involved" at school;*

6. *Students with "highly involved" resident fathers were less likely to repeat a grade; and*

7. *Students with non-resident fathers who participated in even one activity at school were 39 percent less likely to repeat a grade and 50 percent less likely to be suspended or expelled, and slightly more likely to participate in extracurricular activities.*

In addition, the survey determined that higher father involvement at school was closely linked with the likelihood a child would be involved in community activities and that he or she would go on to college. Interestingly, the positive effect of fathers' involvement held true regardless of the level of mothers' participation at school.

Moreover, the report concluded, fathers fill a unique role in their children's educational lives: fathers play more with their children and do so in a more physical manner, apparently fostering the development of analytical skills, especially in their sons. Children were also found to rely more on their fathers for factual information and typically report that fathers and mothers have different educational goals: mothers want them to "feel special and important," while fathers want them to learn and do well academically. "Plausible hypotheses that stem from this research," the report's authors stated, "are that maternal involvement is beneficial for the social and emotional adjustment of children to school, particularly young children, but that *paternal involvement may be the most important for academic achievement*" [our emphasis].

What about fathers' involvement in school when their children are older? The importance of paternal involvement at school actually increases as children get older. The NCES Report specifically noted that middle and high school students with involved fathers were significantly more likely to do better in school and to experience fewer social and emotional difficulties.

This is all well and good, but the purpose of this book is to help *all* parents do their jobs better. If you are a father, by all means get more involved at your children's school. But what if you're a mother? Short of a sex change, what can you do to help your child do better in school? It's difficult to say, because so little research has been done regarding *why* fathers' involvement in school makes such a dramatic difference. Theories abound: Most fathers are involved so little that those who make the effort make a strong impression on their children; having two parents rather than one beating the drum about academic achievement motivates children to do better in school; children listen to their fathers regarding the importance of academic achievement because they are typically the main breadwinner in the family.

The truth is that no one knows exactly what it is about a father's involvement in school that makes such a powerful difference to his children's performance. There has been some research on what fathers do differently that can provide some guidance. For example, when helping their children with homework, fathers are more likely to expect the children to find the answer themselves, even when it is difficult. This is entirely consistent with the findings of Kyle Pruett that we discussed at the opening of the chapter.

We speculate that a substantial part of the effect is tied to the specific ways in which fathers express different expectations about their children's success in school. Every parent can adopt some of these strategies by doing the following:

1. Set high expectations for your child's *effort* in school.

Make certain that your child understands that you expect her to work hard and try her best. Don't let her take delight in what comes easily and let the rest slide. Especially when children are just starting to learn the basics, it's important to let them know that hard work can make up for a lack of natural ability.

2. Set high expectations for your child's *performance* in school.

If your child is reading novels in kindergarten, expect him to improve his reading comprehension or speed by first grade. If your first grader still can't understand adding and subtracting, let him know that you expect him to master the concepts by a certain point in the school year.

3. Emphasize homework.

There's a great debate in many areas about "too much homework." The truth is that most American children spend far too little time studying at home. Set aside a time and place for homework. Ask them about their homework every day. If they don't have any, assign it yourself. Help them (this does not mean doing it for them) or at least check over the result (this does not mean correcting it, only being aware if they are having trouble with a major concept).

4. Teach to the test.

Like it or not, much of your children's academic success will depend on their test-taking performance. Know when tests are taking place and help your child study. Go over tests and help them with weak areas so they can improve the next time.

5. Nurture frustration.

This sounds counter-intuitive, but you must teach your child to encounter frustration and work past it. Put aside your own feelings and make sure this important lesson is learned.

6. Support the teacher.

Too many parents are ready to blame the teacher when classroom problems develop. There are some bad apples, but the vast majority of teachers are hard working and dedicated. Get to know them at the beginning of the year and make it clear that academic performance is a priority in your home. Stay in touch via conferences, voice mail, and e-mail to head off any problems before they get out of control.

Expectations Regarding Athletics and Other Activities

Participation in sports has always been a special part of American childhood, but the number of children involved in organized athletic programs has exploded over the past twenty years. It is estimated that from 30 to 45 million children ages six through eighteen participate in at least one school or community-based athletic program. And the age at which children first participate in sports is continuing to drop.

The guiding principle for expectations regarding athletic and other activities should be that *school comes first*. Nothing is more important for our children's future happiness than a good education, and we should tell them that in strong terms as often as possible.

That said, there is tremendous value to be gained from involvement in sports and other extracurricular activities, including music, art, theater, forensics, and business. We should all expect our children to be involved in athletics, if only for reasons of their physical health. We are all aware of the depressing statistics regarding child inactivity and obesity. Involvement in athletics and other extracurricular activities can also teach teamwork, sportsmanship, and perseverance.

Our role as concerned parents is to help our children find an activity that they enjoy and help them succeed. That often means trying a lot of things that they don't, and walking the fine line between supporting our children and letting them quit without trying hard enough. It also means helping them limit their extracurricular activities, budget their time, and generally learn to balance all of the demands in their young lives.

Here's a warning: we all know that athletic participation can be a wonderful experience in the lives of our children. But more and more commentators have pointed to serious problems as well: commercialization, the decline of sportsmanship, and the use of drugs to enhance performance, to name only a few. It is no secret that today's sports entertainment industry actively glorifies a lifestyle in which sex and alcohol play a central role. As parents we must all take care to make sure that our children absorb the best, and avoid the worst, that our sports culture has to offer.

There is another problem with the sports culture that hits much closer to home: fathers who permit sports to become their primary connection with their children. Sports, of course, have always been an important way for fathers to spend time with their children. Indeed, sports columnist Brian Churney has written that "[s]ports and fathers just seem to go together, like apple pie and ice cream. And, in fact, few of us can imagine doing one without the other."

While most fathers have only good intentions when they encourage their children to participate in organized sports, it's easy for the activity to crowd out more important things about their relationship, even to replace a healthy relationship altogether. We all owe it to our children to make sure that our joint participation in sports is an outgrowth of a strong, loving relationship with them, not a substitute for it.

Expectations Regarding Adulthood

Earlier we mentioned how we can have expectations about our children's behavior, but only hopes regarding outcomes. We're all familiar with the parents' cliché: "I don't care if you decide to be a ditch digger, just be a good one." This is a great approach. Dr. William Sears has warned that "[i]t's important that your expectations about your child's talents and direction in life are realistic. You want your children to be all they can be, not just what you want them to be." He advises parents to employ the "whatever you do, do it well" approach with their children.

Though we have been conditioned to pretend that all we want is for our children to be happy, the truth is that many of us have very detailed visions of what our grown children will be like. It's only natural. After all, everything we do with them, and everything we teach them, is geared toward producing a certain kind of adult.

None of us want to raise an adult who chews with his mouth open, never says please or thank you, kicks small animals while walking down the street, or winds up in jail. But our expectations go much further. Most of us expect our children to complete high school, college, or even graduate school. We expect our children to support themselves and to behave in a socially acceptable fashion (most of the time). We may expect them to marry and have children or to make a lot of money or have a prestigious job (the latter two don't necessarily go together).

Are these expectations bad? On the contrary, they are absolutely necessary. Much of what we teach our children when they are young is precisely to prepare them for the adulthood we envision. A society in which parents genuinely had no expectations for the type of adults their children would become would be a scary place indeed.

That's not to say that expectations can't get out of control. Some parents have such high or specific expectations that they end up stifling their children's success and happiness.

> *Kevin: I knew a girl in college whose parents had made it clear from a young age that they wanted her to become a doctor. She worked hard and made the grades, but once in college she became frustrated and disillusioned. She really wanted to become a nurse, not so far from what her parents wanted, but parental and cultural pressure made her too scared to tell them.*

Or consider expectations about family. So many young people are afraid to tell their parents they're gay because it doesn't fit with their expectations: A son- or daughter-in-law, children, a house with a picket fence. A same-sex partner in an urban loft with a child resulting from an implanted surrogate may not be what they have in mind.

The key to expectations about adulthood is not to eliminate them. Instead, it's to make your children understand that you will love and support them even if they don't end up exactly the way you'd hoped.

Keeping Expectations Reasonable

It's no secret that many fathers (and mothers) who expect a great deal from their children set the bar so high that the result is counter-productive: discouragement, burnout, even rebellion. In her book *The Everything Parents Guide to Raising a Successful Child,* Denise Witmer notes that children are most likely to meet their parents' expectations when they are *reasonable* and *consistent.* Indeed, keeping expectations reasonable is central to successful expectation parenting. The goal is to set expectations that will challenge your child to perform to her fullest without discouraging her from trying.

How do you make sure that your expectations are reasonable? Expectations are reasonable when they take into account a child's developmental readiness, when you are prepared to follow through on them, and when they are flexible enough to be changed. Let's discuss each of these elements briefly.

Some expectations are reasonable for all but a few children: Be polite, clean up after yourself, finish your homework, be kind to animals. Other expectations are reasonable for only a handful of children: become expert at the violin, be first in your class, become an Eagle Scout, attend an Ivy League graduate school. It all depends on the individual child and your own family.

No expectation can be reasonable unless it takes into account the developmental readiness of each individual child. Again, simple things like politeness at the table and saying thank you for presents and visits are all right for just about every child. But be careful when you start thinking about chores, school performance, and sports. Is your child a whiz at math? If so, then expecting top grades in algebra is reasonable. Does your child have poor coordination? If that's the case, then expecting her to become a soccer star is not reasonable. You know your children best, so you are in the best position to decide what they can handle.

But remember: just because you have an exceptionally talented, high-achieving child, don't assume that higher and higher expectations are always appropriate. In his book *Positive Pushing: How to Raise a Successful and Happy Child,* Jim Taylor makes a canny distinction between pursuing excellence and perfectionism. He writes that the former means being successful most of the time, "an achievable and worthwhile goal toward which you should encourage your child to strive." By contrast, the latter is unattainable and fruitless, and pursuing it can turn your child into a neurotic who can never be happy or satisfied with her success. Do your children a favor: Emphasize excellence and pooh-pooh perfectionism!

Treating each child differently has the potential to create problems among siblings. Susie may wonder why she has to do more advanced work than Harold. Chuck may bristle when Claire is heaped with praise for something he mastered when he was years younger. Confront these problems with honesty. Explain to your children exactly what you are doing and why. It is a rare family in which one child is superior in every way to his brothers and sisters. Each child has strengths and weaknesses, and it is only fair to take them into account in formulating your expectations.

Your expectations would mean little, and could hardly be termed reason-

Internalizing Expectations

As parents, we all know that we won't always be around to make decisions for our children. Consequently, one of our primary tasks is to teach our children to think for themselves. This is certainly true when it comes to expectations. Even as we take the time to formulate and communicate expectations to our children, we should be aware that all of our efforts will amount to very little if our children don't learn to set their own expectations for themselves.

As our children grow, our role in setting expectations for them should give way to our children setting expectations for themselves. This is part of the larger journey children undergo to making mature choices. Writing in *Positive Pushing*, Jim Taylor advises that treating expectations as choices your child can make may actually increase the likelihood that she will meet them. "[T]he responsibility for meeting the expectations is her own, and this sense of ownership motivates your child to meet the expectations."

You can encourage this process. Once you are satisfied that your child is comfortable with the notion of expectations and the process you have created for formulating and communicating your expectations, start asking her what she expects of herself. Be specific. Ask "why do you want to do this?" And "how do you hope this will turn out?" By asking these questions you can help your child learn how to formulate her own expectations.

You can help this process further by supporting your child in her expectations. Does she want to write a novel? You might find a book that describes the process and how to get started. Lend your help when things get difficult. Your backup will be important in the early stages. Then, as your child gets older, you'll need to help less and less. Remember, you're a source of support even if your child sets an expectation that you don't understand.

Molly, the nine-year-old daughter of Dave, one of our father panelists, is already internalizing the positive lesson of high expectations. "Molly has set swimming goals for herself," Dave says, "and learning to set goals early in life will set a pattern for future goal setting in other endeavors, and this is setting herself up for future success."

If you are successful in creating a culture of expectation in your home, you'll end up with a goal-oriented teenager who knows how to set her own expectations with little or no guidance from you. And when she fails to meet her own expectations, you'll find that she can be much harder on herself than you would even consider.

able, if you were not prepared to follow through on them. Contrary to what you might think, following through on an unmet expectation does not necessarily mean punishment. Most often it will mean that you'll express your disappointment (often surprisingly powerful) and then help pinpoint the problem and help your child overcome it.

Part and parcel of follow-through is consistency, something we mentioned earlier. Consistency is a simple concept: it means doing something the same way every time. In the context of expectations, there are two types of consistency you should be concerned with: internal consistency and outcome consistency. Internal consistency means making sure that your expectations make sense in relation to one another. Outcome consistency refers to the practice of reacting to your child's performance the same way every time.

The final element of reasonableness is *flexibility*. Make a commitment to be flexible enough to change your expectations when circumstances warrant, and understand that you'll always be formulating new expectations as your children grow. Your child may decide that the hockey team is taking too much time away from school and friends. Don't insist that he stay on the team because of your expectation that he will become a top-level hockey player (unless you're concerned about a pattern of quitting difficult things). Be flexible; let him drop hockey, perhaps with the understanding that he will replace it with a less demanding organized, extracurricular activity.

The simple fact that your children are constantly growing will also demand flexibility in your expectations. Expecting your daughter to keep up with her volunteer group now that she's juggling several advanced placement courses may not make sense. Nor should you insist that your son continue to play trucks with his little brother now that he's in middle school.

Your own growth will also create occasions for flexibility. Ideally, we are all continuing to learn even as adults. Have the courage and self-awareness to incorporate your learning into your expectations. We know of one father who decided that he was pushing his son to participate in athletics largely to satisfy his own love of sports. Once his priorities had changed and he realized he had to spend more time with his children, he let his son decide whether to continue in sports.

Make Love a Constant

No one benefits if children feel that they will no longer be loved if they fail to meet their parents' expectations, no matter how reasonable. But your love for your children should not be entirely unconditional, regardless of what you might read in other parenting books. What is a time-out, after all? It is a punishment that places a child away from his parents' love for a defined period. Although it may make some of us uncomfortable to think about it in this way, all punishment involves conditional love.

Conditional love is an essential part of expectation parenting as long as you are careful about its deployment. For example, you should condition your love on your child demonstrating the values that are most important in your family. You may also condition your love for your older child on her participating as a contributing member of society. It is your responsibility to demonstrate your strong disapproval for her actions. Remember Dave, the father who expected his daughter to push herself to do her best in swimming? He's found a good balance, tempering his high expectations with love. "If she falls down I expect her to get back up. I do give her sympathy, but I also let her know she's tough and can handle anything if she keeps her head up and does her best. I'm always proud of her regardless of the results, and she knows that I'm always on her side."

The Power of Your Example

Surveys of high school students repeatedly reveal that their greatest heroes are their parents and grandparents. We as parents often forget what towering figures we are to our children, even long after they have gone out on their own. This is strange, because we are all children, too, and we all know the power that a word or two from our mother or father can carry. All the expectations in the world, no matter how carefully formulated and well communicated, will mean nothing in the face of a bad example. "Do as I say, not as I do" has a place in parenting (that's another book), but it's not good practice over the long term. The best thing we can do for our children is to live the way we hope they will live, with kindness, integrity, and love.

7

Parenting as Partners

Incorporating Fatherstyle Every Day

" A team effort is a lot of people doing what I say. "

—Michael Winner, British film director

There is a fundamental truth about parenting that goes unmentioned most of the time: it is a job typically done by two people with wildly divergent backgrounds, styles, and even basic beliefs. As we noted in the Introduction, the goal of this book has never been to prove that mothers are doing a poor job of parenting, nor to argue that fathers are better parents than mothers. Instead, our aim throughout has been to bring some much-needed balance to parenting advice by demonstrating that involved fathers have a lot to say about good parenting.

In her groundbreaking bestseller *You Just Don't Understand,* Deborah Tannen wrote that men and women have "different, but equally valid styles" of communicating. She concluded her book by noting that both sexes should be flexible enough to try each other's styles in order to avoid the problems of miscommunication. Tannen's book and its sequels helped spark awareness of gender-based differences in everyday behavior.

With appropriate modifications, a similar paradigm can be used to describe the parenting styles of most men and most women. As we've seen in our discussion so far, men and women have (generally) very different approaches to the challenges of parenthood. *Both are valid*, and we should be flexible enough to adopt some elements of each other's styles in order to become better parents.

Accordingly, in this final chapter we'll show parents how they can combine their different styles of parenting to raise confident and caring kids while becoming happier parents at the same time. We'll explain how fatherstyle can be integrated into the shared parenting experienced by most families today. We will briefly review and summarize each of the five elements of fatherstyle and discuss the specific ways couples can use these elements to improve their parenting as a team. Using real-world examples taken from our workshops, we will identify some of the common conflicts that arise from differing parenting styles and how mothers and fathers can recognize them.

This chapter will also feature an extended examination of three fictional, composite couples facing parenting challenges. We will discuss the differences in their parenting styles and their frustrations with continuing parenting problems. Then we'll explain how the fatherstyle framework can be applied to address their specific challenges and solve their parenting dilemmas.

It Takes Two

Parenting is more of a team effort than any time in recent memory. With the vast majority of mothers in the work force and changing expectations for fathers, men and women are increasingly sharing the duties of parenting. At the beginning of this book we cited studies and surveys demonstrating that fathers spend significantly more time parenting than they did twenty years ago. While many readers may legitimately grouse that mothers still spend more time on parenting and juggling the competing demands of work and home, there is no question that fathers are doing more every year.

Even accounting for demographic trends that favor single-parent families, most children are still raised by two parents who are married to each other. Like it or not, parents must both participate in child rearing. This is the first and foremost reason that parents should learn to become an effective team. There are other reasons, too. Two heads *are* better than one. A central premise of this book is that mothers and fathers each have something different and valuable to offer to the practice of parenting. It naturally follows that children do best when they have two active parents. Not only does each parent bring a unique perspective to the problems of parenting, both moms and dads get a better idea of what the problems are when they're both involved.

For example, many of the behavior problems a mother experiences may have very little to do with the child and everything to do with how she's handling the discipline. A traditional couple might never find that out because dad never spends enough time alone with his child to see the difference his style can make. A parenting team will see this immediately and check it before it gets out of hand.

A third reason for taking steps to work together as parents is that, as a team, you and your spouse can present a united front to your children. Even the sweetest kids ask mom when dad says no (and vice versa) and try to play their parents against each other. This behavior can never be eliminated, but team parenting can cut it down considerably. Parents who work together will be enforcing the same rules and will both be on board when discipline has to be meted out.

Finally, parenting as a team is guaranteed to strengthen your marriage. Experts say money is the number one cause of conflict in marriages, but our experience tells us that disagreements about parenting can't be far behind. Especially for many fathers, when they feel that their input is not required or that their views are being actively ignored, they will disengage from parenting. This result is bad for parents and children alike.

Assessing Your Situation

Before you can go about creating a team parenting approach to fatherstyle you have to make an honest assessment of your current parenting situation. As we see it, there are three primary possibilities: You and your spouse are both committed to adopting a fatherstyle approach; you are the only one who is interested in making the effort; or your spouse voices support but expects you to do virtually all of the work. There is a fourth possibility, of course; your spouse may be gung ho and you are the foot dragger, but we assume that you wouldn't be reading this book if that were the case.

Don't make the mistake of assuming that you already know your situation. Make a point of taking about it with your spouse. You've now read enough of this book to explain generally what it's all about. Ask your spouse whether he or she is interested in working with you to make changes in your parenting. You might be surprised by the response.

If you and your spouse are both committed to changing your parenting for the better, you're very lucky and the next section is written for you. If you fall into either of the latter two categories, you should skip the next sections (temporarily) and go directly to the section entitled "Going It Alone."

Understanding Your Differing Styles

Before you and your spouse can learn to work together as a team, you have to learn more about your different parenting styles. Most of us, of course, are well aware that we parent differently than our spouses (or that we would if given the chance). Mary knows that Ken prefers to play outside with the kids, while she prefers to read to them. Henry understands that Melissa doesn't know how to control their children in the period between dinner and bedtime, but it's easy for him. Jenna has learned that Bill can't stand it when the kids run around the house screaming, but she views it as a healthy release of energy. And on and on.

Some of the most common differences in parenting styles are as follows:

1. strict *vs.* permissive
2. involved *vs.* hands-off
3. friend *vs.* parent
4. emotional *vs.* intellectual

The differences in this list are familiar to all of us. Nevertheless, few of us are aware of *why* they exist. It's essential that you figure this out before you decide how you and your spouse will integrate your parenting styles into a unified approach. We've designed a short quiz to help you get started. You and your spouse should take this quiz before you continue with the rest of this section.

Once you've compared your responses to our parenting quiz, you can develop a better understanding of what motivates your different parenting styles. The quiz, of course, is hardly a scientific exercise or a serious diagnostic tool. Instead, it's designed to generate discussion. Take an hour one evening or weekend to compare and talk about the results. The goal is twofold: To help you and your spouse learn more about how and why you parent differently, and to determine what parenting issues are most important to each of you. This includes issues that have yet to become important, perhaps because your children are not old enough to confront them.

Discussing parenting styles with your spouse is important. For example, Don and Liz may learn that they don't see eye to eye on whether their children, now toddlers, should be permitted to walk or bike to friends' houses or the park by themselves when they're older. This reflects a general difference of opinion on how much freedom children should be allowed. Kate and Michael may discover that they disagree regarding whether their middle-school-age children should attend sleepaway camp. This stems from different upbringings and attitudes toward long separations between parents and children. And Georgette and Sam may determine that one believes in after-school jobs for high schoolers and the other doesn't. Again, being raised in starkly varying circumstances has led to their disagreement.

The idea at this stage is not to discuss (or argue) until you reach a consensus, or until one spouse simply gives up. Rather, you're on a fact-finding mission. Try to cover as many areas as possible. If you have trouble getting a discussion started, return to the quiz and talk about your answers to a specific question. Then discuss each of the other questions in turn. You may even want to take notes so that you don't have to revisit any topics you've already covered.

Once you've spent a few hours on this exercise, each of you should have an understanding of the other's parenting style. You may even learn something about your own style. On the most basic level, are you a parent who believes in letting the kids do their own thing, or do you prefer to impose order and control? Do you think the kids come first and your relationship second, or are you intent on tending your marriage first?

You'll find that your answers to these broad questions of style will almost

Parenting Style Quiz

Take this quiz and then find out what it shows about your parenting style by using the guide at the end.

1. You hear your child begin to cry in the next room. You

a) Rush to pick her up, hug her close, and comfort her.

b) Let her cry for a few minutes before intervening.

c) Ignore it because your spouse is home.

d) Consult a mental checklist to determine the cause of the crying and how to stop it.

2. When your child is sleeping, you

a) Gaze at him adoringly for at least twenty minutes.

b) Throw in a load of laundry and pick up the house.

c) Watch the game.

d) Organize his baby pictures into albums for relatives.

3. Your child is a late walker. You

a) Let her know that there's no pressure to perform on an arbitrary schedule.

b) Mention it to the pediatrician and ask his advice.

c) Tell your spouse that your daughter will walk when she's good and ready.

d) Schedule an evaluation with a specialist and start a physical therapy regimen.

4. You're a firm believer that discipline

a) Is for families who do not show their children enough love.

b) Is an important way to set boundaries and teach self-control.

c) Is best administered starting from the bottom.

d) Should only be imposed as part of a consistent parenting plan.

5. Your cousin gives your son a doll for his birthday. You

a) Thank her for helping your son develop his nurturing side.

b) Place it with all of his other toys.

c) Wait until she leaves to throw it out.

d) Watch your son with the doll to determine whether he is left-brained or right-brained.

6. You spend thirty minutes a day of alone time with your child. During this time you

a) Get on the floor and do whatever she directs you to do.

b) Suggest a game that you both enjoy.

c) Watch videos of your favorite childhood show.

d) Use flash cards to develop her reading skills.

7. Your child expresses reluctance to go to school one morning. You

a) Tell him he can stay home if he doesn't like it anymore.

b) File it away in case it becomes a regular thing.

c) Tell him he has to go to school whether he likes it or not.

d) Talk to the teacher about whether there's a problem in the classroom.

8. When you take your young child for an overnight at your parents' house, you

a) Make sure to bring his favorite blanket, pillow case, toys, stuffed animals, and books.

b) Prepare a note with his typical feeding and sleep schedule.

c) Remember the diapers but forget the infant formula.

d) Include a diagram showing how to administer the Heimlich maneuver to a baby.

9. You are already planning to

a) Form a Daisy troop for your daughter and serve as group leader.

b) Adjust your work schedule to help out in your child's classroom once a semester.

c) Coach your son's traveling football team.

d) Buy an extreme sports-grade bicycle helmet for your child's fourth birthday.

10. You secretly worry that someday your child

a) Will want to attend a private school outside of your neighborhood.

b) Will have trouble adjusting to school.

c) Won't be part of the "in" crowd.

d) Will do so poorly in her AP courses that she'll have to attend a public university.

11. You think the right time to talk to your child about drugs is

a) When you're dropping her off at college.

b) When the anti-drug curriculum is introduced in school.

c) When she tells you her friends are really into pot.

d) When she points out someone smoking at the mall.

12. Your son's teacher says he is bullying younger kids. You

a) Take him to counseling to help him control his aggressive impulses.

b) Punish him and explain the importance of being sensitive to others.

c) Tell the teacher someone else must have started it.

d) Start boxing lessons so he can learn to fight the right way.

13. Your child consistently forgets to put her dirty clothes in the hamper. You

a) Offer to get her a jazzier hamper to help her remember.

b) Refuse to launder any clothes not in the hamper.

c) Burn any dirty clothes found on the floor of her room.

d) Ground her for a week and force her to do her own laundry for a month.

14. Your fifth-grade son is invited to a sleepover that will feature an R-rated video. You

a) Have a talk to help him get as much out of the movie as possible.

b) Explain that he can join the party after the movie.

c) Decide it's O.K. when you learn the rating reflects violence, not sex.

d) Forbid him from attending the party or seeing his friends again.

15. Your middle school daughter complains that all her friends have cell phones. You

a) Get her one that matches yours so you can send more text messages.

b) Remind her that she'll get a cell phone as soon as she starts to drive.

c) Tell her that she won't find a way to talk to boys that easily.

d) Get her one on the condition that she

use it to monitor her stock portfolio.

16. The high school math teacher suggests your daughter join the honors class. You

a) *Tell her but explain that it might mean giving up her clog dancing lessons.*

b) *Review the honors math text and talk with her about whether she can handle it.*

c) *Don't mention it because boys don't like brainy girls.*

d) *Voice your disappointment that the invitation didn't come sooner.*

17. Your high school-age son wants money to go on a spring break trip to Mexico. You

a) *Give him a little extra and make sure he packs his sunscreen.*

b) *Tell him he's too young to take a trip on his own.*

c) *Make him earn the money and recommend a good brand of condom.*

d) *Insist he stay home to complete some extra tutoring for the SAT.*

18. Your children throw you a surprise fiftieth birthday party. You

a) *Sob so uncontrollably you induce an asthma attack.*

b) *Are so touched you write them each a letter telling them how happy they make you.*

c) *Paste on a fake smile and let them know later you hoped no one would remember.*

d) *Exchange all your presents to buy a piano and lessons for the whole family.*

19. You hope your child grows up to be

a) *Sensitive to others and the environment.*

b) *Happy.*

c) *Successful.*

d) *Rich enough to afford a good therapist.*

20. The thing you are looking forward to most is .

a) *Helping your child make the world a better place.*

b) *Getting to know your child as she grows.*

c) *Helping your child achieve what you never could.*

d) *Proving once and for all that nurture beats nature every time.*

SCORING AND ASSESSMENT

Mostly (a) answers: You're a very soft touch. You care very much about your child's welfare and are committed to doing *anything* to make your child happier.

Mostly (b) answers: You're sensible and measured. You care about your child and about being a successful parent, but you know you don't have all the answers and you're willing to ask for help.

Mostly (c) answers: You're a real throwback. You're happy to stick with the old parenting roles. You don't seem to understand (or care) how times have changed, and you're generally unwilling to alter your approach accordingly.

Mostly (d) answers: You're an obsessive hyper-parent. The success of your children is very important to you. You've invested a lot of your own ego and self-esteem into your children's performance in life.

always determine the positions each of you will take on the dozens (hundreds!) of specific parenting issues that you will confront over the years. We are careful to say *almost* because even the most dogmatic parent will occasionally take positions that seem inconsistent with his or her general style. Be careful not to mistake understanding for pigeonholing. You and your spouse both deserve the freedom to treat each problem as it comes.

Accepting Your Differences

Understanding is one thing, accepting is another. While most of us have a general idea of the ways in which we parent differently than our spouses, few of us accept these differences. This isn't much of a problem when one spouse is doing virtually all the parenting. But team parenting won't work when one spouse refuses to accept the other spouse's style, believing it to be somehow illegitimate or even harmful.

When we speak of accepting your differences, however, we don't mean simply doing everything your spouse's way. We mean respecting their different parenting style and being open to incorporating it into your joint parenting efforts. Make certain that you and your spouse accept each other's style before you go any further. Otherwise, your effort at team parenting will be both brief and disastrous.

The Fatherstyle Framework

Now that you and your spouse understand and accept each other's different parenting styles, you are ready to tackle the fatherstyle framework. The fatherstyle framework is a cooperative, gender-based approach for integrating your different parenting styles using the elements of fatherstyle. In this section we will explain how you and your spouse can use this framework to formulate positions on common parenting problems, such as whining, failure to do chores, backtalk, and refusal to participate in family activities. We'll show you how to turn your positions into scripts, how to use the scripts to respond to varied situations, and how to revise your approach after evaluating feedback from the results of your efforts.

The Fatherstyle Framework consists of seven steps:

1. *scheduling*
2. *discussing*
3. *agreeing*
4. *formulating*
5. *scripting*
6. *experimenting*
7. *revising*

Each step follows from the one before. They can be completed over a long period of time, addressing many issues at once, or they can be completed for one issue at a time. It's up to you and your spouse.

Let's discuss each step in turn.

Scheduling.

Scheduling means setting aside a regular time to discuss parenting matters. This is the most important step of all, because you will accomplish nothing if you don't get to discuss the subjects that are important to you. If it's impossible for you to set aside a regular time each week or month, make sure you agree that you *will* talk at a specific time to schedule your discussions. For example, if you and your wife have a habit of talking about the coming week while watching television on Sunday evenings, use that time to decide when you will have your parenting pow-wow.

Discussing.

Discussing refers to using your scheduled time to voice issues and talk over problems. Don't necessarily put anything in writing (unless your memories are so bad that neither of you will remember what was said a few days later), but do come prepared with a list of topics if you find that helpful. Our experience is that a list can sometimes facilitate productive discussion, especially when it might be awkward to raise a subject.

Your goal at this stage is to identify the issues that concern each of you. It may come as news to your spouse that you've been worried about your son's addiction to video games. You may be surprised to learn that your spouse wants your daughter to be more involved in organized extracurricular activities. Discussion is the only way to find these things out.

Agreeing.

Agreeing means concluding your discussion by adopting a common approach that addresses and incorporates each person's concerns. As with any compromise, both of you should expect to come away feeling that you gave up something important. The idea is not to bludgeon your spouse until he or she gives in to your point of view. If your attitude is that you're right and you won't budge, you'll never come to an agreement. Give a little to get a little there, however, and you'll find that you and your spouse can agree on a joint approach.

If you are unable to reach agreement on something important, don't let it bog you down. Do what diplomats do: put it aside and address it again later. You may even decide to push some issues off to a later session. There's no law that says you must resolve everything in one evening. In fact, taking things one step at a time is more realistic and usually more effective.

In the meantime, focus on the things that are going well. Once you've got a long list of things you agree on, the combination of good will and momentum will help you resolve the last few points in dispute. Keep at it until you've reached agreement on everything.

Formulating.

Formulating means moving from a general agreement about how to proceed to a specific strategy of action. This is perhaps the most difficult step. Reaching agreement about a general approach, while challenging, often pales alongside the prospect of turning the agreement into a viable approach.

How do you go about doing it? Rather than start by talking about the problem, talk about the cause instead. For example, say you're addressing your daughter's extreme lack of table manners. You and your spouse agree that they are atrocious and need immediate improvement. Your first instinct might be to make a mental list of all her offenses: chewing with her mouth open, wiping her mouth with her sleeve, eating with her fingers, etc. But this is too narrow. Ask yourselves why she eats that way. Perhaps she has so little time to eat lunch at school that she's gotten into the habit of rushing through meals. Maybe your family rarely eats together at the table, or she's ravenous after soccer practice. Perhaps she's never been to a nice restaurant where good manners are expected. Or maybe it's all of these things put together. Now your strategy reveals itself: more family meals, a snack after soccer practice, and occasional restaurant meals. It might just work.

Scripting.

Scripting does not refer to writing and memorizing lines. Instead, it means turning your strategy into a step-by-step plan to address the parenting issues you are facing. You must anticipate the possible pitfalls and head them off. For example, you and your spouse may decide that you're going to tackle your daughter's persistent absent-mindedness about her class assignments by requiring her to keep a planner and a corresponding desk calendar which she must consult at specific times each day. Your script for this approach would include what you'll require her to do and when, how and when you'll present your plan to her, how you'll monitor her progress, and what you'll do when she either succeeds or fails.

We've included a sample script on the opposite page.

Experimenting.

Experimenting means implementing your scripted plans in everyday life with your children. The emphasis is on actual situations. The idea is not to create a conflict or sit your children down for a talk on a particular subject. Instead, your task is to tell your child about what you're doing in a non-confrontational fashion and then try it out. Experimenting works best when it starts small, say, with new rules about household chores, and steadily expands to include more serious (and combustible) issues such as dating.

Sample Script

In the text we explained that *scripting* means turning your strategy for addressing a parenting problem into a step-by-step plan. Aside from changing your child's behavior, your goal in scripting is to anticipate and avoid potential problems with your strategy. The following sample contains all of the essential elements of a successful script: your plan of action, how and when you'll present your plan to your child, how you'll monitor his progress, and what you'll do when he either succeeds or fails. Use this as a guide only; it's not intended to reflect the nuances you'll confront when addressing an actual parenting problem.

Problem: Failure to clean up before bedtime each evening.

Plan of Action: Require child to clean up designated areas and items at a specific time each evening.

Presentation of Plan: Discussion and written note on Tuesday after dinner.

Monitoring: Dad will decide whether clean up is done adequately each evening.

Follow-up Action: First failure will result in loss of computer privileges for one day. Second failure will result in loss of computer privileges for a week. Each additional failure will result in loss of computer and television privileges for one week. Continuing failures will result in another discussion and a revised plan of action.

That's all there is to it. If you think it's necessary, write out your script and post it on the refrigerator or family bulletin board. Consult it every day until you see appropriate results. If things are not going well, follow the remaining steps in the fatherstyle framework.

You can follow this simple format or create one of your own. The important thing is not what your script looks like, but that it contain all the information you need to follow through on the problem. It will also provide a record of what you and your spouse agreed to do in the event that there are questions later.

Some parents may find the idea of a script silly or overly directive. This is your family, after all, not General Motors. But we think recording your plan is essential to the process of identifying and addressing the parenting issues that you and your spouse care most about. Without a script, you'll find yourselves falling into the same routines that created your problems in the first place.

Revising.

Revising means changing your strategies and plans in response to their effectiveness or lack of effectiveness in practice. Expect to do a lot of revising. Parenting is a learning process, after all. It may turn out that you were dead wrong about why your son was slacking off in algebra, or your plan to require an hour of math homework every night is actually making the problem worse. Maybe that habit your daughter has of playing her music loud after dinner has nothing to do with a plot to annoy you. Your chore chart may cause such resentment that your children end up doing less around the house than they did before you implemented your plan.

The key to effective revision is to keep your eye on the ball. Don't get caught up in why your plan failed. Change it, get rid of it, do whatever it takes, but remember the problem that led to the plan in the first place. Do some new formulating and make a new plan. Whatever you do, don't give up!

Dealing with Conflicts

No matter how cooperative you and your spouse manage to be, conflicts will inevitably arise on parenting as a team. Not surprisingly, most of the conflicts couples confront arise from a clash in parenting styles. The best way to deal with conflict, of course, is to avoid it in the first place. To that end, we've compiled a list of ten guidelines for avoiding conflict with your spouse over parenting issues. Each item is followed by examples of how to (and how not to) handle situations that present themselves every day.

1. Don't Make Your Spouse the Bad Guy.

Remember the classic warning "Wait Till Your Father Gets Home"? It became such a common refrain in American households that there was even a short-lived situation comedy with that title. Times have changed to the point that "Wait till your mother gets home" is probably heard in some homes, too. The tendency of mothers to force fathers into the role of disciplinarian is deplorable, and one we touched upon when we were discussing discipline. It bears repeating. It is not fair to make your spouse the bad guy, no matter what your motivation. Often, such a destructive division of responsibilities holds one parent hostage to the other's poor parenting. And we're not just talking about discipline. There are any number of situations in which one parent, perhaps exhausted from saying no all the time or simply unwilling to appear mean to the children, makes the other parent the bad guy either explicitly or by subtly undermining his point of view in front of the children.

Not this: *You go to your room and wait until your father gets home. You'll get quite a punishment when he hears what you did.*
This: *You go to your room until dinner time. Your father and I will discuss what happened and we'll let you know what your punishment will be in the morning.*

Not this: *I'd love to get a puppy. It's your mother who's against it.*
This: *Your mother and I don't think it's the right time to get a puppy. We'll discuss it again after your next birthday.*

2. Always Present a United Front.

This is an oldie but a goodie. This rule was common sense when we were all growing up, but a lot of parents today have forgotten its wisdom. Whether it's because there are so many more decisions to make about our children's lives, or because we have less time to talk about parenting dilemmas, more and more couples are staking out different positions—*and letting the kids know it*. It would be hard to imagine a more egregious error. Your children will run circles around you and your spouse if you don't back each other up. This means pretending to agree with your spouse even when you're caught unaware.

One sound way to build a united front is to take parenting classes together. One of the members of our fathers panel and his wife took a class that emphasized letting their children make choices and live with the consequences of their mistakes. He believes that it has helped them stick together and support each other, using these techniques. "Because we have this united strategy, we have very few real disagreements when it comes to the major parenting challenges."

And the importance of a united front doesn't just apply in the house. Your united front must extend to friends and, especially, relatives. Resist the urge to tell your mother how wrong your spouse is when it comes to discipline, or you'll suffer the consequences longer than you can imagine.

Not this: *I don't think your dad understands how important this is to you. Go ahead to the party and I'll handle the fallout.*
This: *I don't care how important this party is to you. Your father said no, and that means no from both of us.*

Not this: *You know how your mother feels about jeans at school. I know it's silly, but we have to go along with it.*
This: *The rule is no jeans at school. Period.*

3. Resolve Disagreements in Private.
This is a necessary corollary of the previous rule. After all, you and your spouse are likely to disagree frequently about any number of things. When you do, do it outside of your children's presence. That doesn't mean you have to hide the fact that you disagree. Far from it. Just make sure your children know that your disagreements are none of their business.

Not this: *Now, Pat, that's too harsh. Why don't we let him go to practice and then finish his homework?*
This: *You heard your mother. No soccer practice until that homework is done.*

Not this: *Don't yell at him like that. He didn't mean to spill the juice.*
This: *Get that juice cleaned up and be more careful next time.*

4. Let Your Spouse Parent His (or Her) Own Way.
Throughout the book we've emphasized that most mothers and fathers have different but equally valid parenting styles. That's a lesson that's easier to hear than to apply in practice. So make sure that your spouse has continuing opportunities to parent his (or her) own way, even if it drives you crazy. Sometimes the best thing to do is just leave the house.

Not this: *That's not how he likes his sandwich. Use grape jelly and cut off the crusts.*
This: *(Silence)*

Not this: *She'll never nap if you get her jazzed up like that.*
This: *I'm going to run some errands this afternoon.*

5. Don't Blame Your Spouse.

Earlier we talked about not turning your spouse into the bad guy. Now we mean something different: Deciding that it's your spouse's fault when something goes wrong with the children. Even if you never say anything (perhaps especially if you never say anything), the idea will fester and lead to more blaming in the future. Your children behave the way they do because of a combination of many factors, but you and your spouse both bear responsibility for the outcome. If you are sure your spouse is to blame for something because he or she does all the parenting, you should start blaming yourself for not living up to your own obligations.

Not this: *She talks like that because you keep giving her that pacifier.*
This: *I've read that speech problems can be related to pacifier use. Let's figure out how to break her of that habit.*

Not this: *His grades are terrible because you never help with his homework.*
This: *Let's switch off with homework. I think he needs another point of view on some of his assignments.*

6. Put Yourself in Your Spouse's Shoes.

Rather than instantly criticizing your spouse, try putting yourself in her (or his) shoes. Think about the pressures and demands she faces each day, all the things she does for the family, and how she might be feeling when parenting challenges occur. If you're lucky, she'll do the same for you.

Not this: *My blue shirt hasn't been washed. What did you do all day?*
This: *You must have had a hard day. Let me throw a load in the washer.*

Not this: *All you ever do is come home and watch television. I have to do everything.*
This: *I know you need to wind down, but I need help with dinner right now.*

7. Respect Your Spouse's Point of View.
Considering that you and your spouse will probably have many disagreements over parenting issues over the years, it only makes sense to respect his or her point of view. This goes beyond a pretense for the sake of the children; we're talking about genuine regard. That means listening and understanding what your spouse has to say and giving it credit. Once you decide that your spouse has no valid opinions on parenting, you'll stop listening and the whole effort will break down.

Not this: *Are you nuts? That's what all the kids are listening to. You're living in the dark ages.*
This: *That's what's popular today, but I understand why it upsets you. Let's figure out some ground rules after the kids are in bed.*

Not this: *You're babying him. Bullies are a fact of life. He needs to learn how to defend himself.*
This: *Let's talk to his teacher and see if this is a real problem. I know we both want him to be O.K.*

8. Give Credit When Credit Is Due.
Everyone likes a pat on the back now and again. Sometimes a kind word is all that gets us through a hard day. Parenting is no different from any other demanding task. Make sure that you take the time to recognize what your spouse does well and mention it. Do this often, especially if you're in the middle of an argument about something else.

Not this: *You keep repeating yourself all the time. Say it once and mean it.*
This: *You handled that really well. I don't think it'll be a problem again.*

Not this: *I'm amazed she didn't get herself killed.*
This: *I'm glad you were there to keep an eye on her. She's so proud of herself now!*

9. Learn from Your Spouse.

The primary goal of this book is to help mothers and fathers become more effective parents by pointing out what they can learn from involved fathers. But that doesn't mean you have to read a book to learn something about parenting. Chances are that your greatest teacher is sitting on the couch next to you. Observe your spouse's interactions with your children and determine what he or she does best. Then try to incorporate that into your own parenting.

Not this: *It's lucky I'm around or they'd never get any culture.*
This: *I've started to play some physical games with them, too. They love it.*

Not this: *Everything's so regimented when you're home. No wonder they rebel.*
This: *The structure really helps them handle the day when they get tired.*

10. Give Your Spouse the Benefit of the Doubt.

This may be the hardest, and most important, lesson of all. Couples face pressures every day. It does no one any good to harp on each other, to complain, or to criticize. You'll find the bumps easier to manage if you remind yourself that everyone (yes, even your spouse) is doing his or her best to get it right. Even on those days when it isn't quite true, maintaining the fiction can make all of our lives a lot easier.

Not this: *How could you forget the dinner? Now we've got nothing and Mitch has karate in an hour.*
This: *Don't worry—we both had long days. I'll order a pizza and we'll have a real family dinner tomorrow.*

Getting to Yes

One of the most valuable resources for pinpointing and resolving differences is the classic *Getting to Yes: Negotiating Agreement Without Giving In* by Roger Fisher, William L. Ury, and William Patton. Fisher's approach, revolutionary when his book was first published, focuses on reaching a "win-win" solution to disputes by understanding the other person's viewpoint and trying to tailor a resolution that takes her concerns into account.

Kevin: *In law school we spent one solid week on nothing but conflict resolution, something that is very important for lawyers to learn. Roger Fisher was a visiting professor at the time, and he spoke to my class in some detail regarding the* Getting to Yes *philosophy. Everyone called him "Dr. Yes."*

Jim: *That must have been fascinating.*

Kevin: *It was. He was an articulate teacher and extremely persuasive, too. A big part of the week was devoted to an exercise in which students divided into opposing teams charged with negotiating a new labor contract for hospital employees. Of course, the whole point was to use the* Getting to Yes *principles in the exercise.*

Jim: *What did you learn?*

Kevin: *Primarily that it's a lot easier to talk about good negotiating than to do it. Fisher told us that the mechanics of all negotiations are essentially the same. I think much of his approach can work to help couples resolve differences over parenting.*

Jim: *Are there any specific techniques couples can use to come to agreement on parenting issues?*

Kevin: *I think so. Fisher's basic framework for negotiating is a series of steps designed to build relationships, create options, and enhance communication between the parties. He emphasizes being "unconditionally constructive." Even if the opponent is acting emotional, balance the emotion with reason. If they misunderstand you, try to understand them. Even if they're not listening, consult them on matters that affect them. Even if they're trying to coerce you, try to persuade them and be open to persuasion. Fisher says that "an agreement is an outcome that each side thinks is better than its best alternative." It sounds simple, but it makes great sense.*

Not this: *You just don't care. I'll be up for hours getting everything ready.*
This: *We can't change that now. Let's both work on it and we'll get it done faster.*

If you still encounter conflicts over parenting issues (and you almost certainly will), the Getting to Yes sidebar has some valuable tips for how you and your spouse can reach common ground even on seemingly intractable issues. If you and your spouse still can't see eye to eye, you might consider starting over or seeking out a therapist or parenting coach.

Going It Alone

The fact that your spouse is unwilling to participate doesn't mean that you can't employ some of the tools we provide in this chapter to improve your parenting. While it's hard to adopt a program of team parenting with no team, much of what we discuss in the prior sections can still be adapted for your use.

For example, take the parenting quiz and use your answers to get a better idea of your parenting style. You may be surprised to find that you think of yourself as a strict parent but you are actually quite lenient. Alternatively, you may discover that you're a bit harder on your kids than you thought. Either way, the exercise will be valuable even without a partner.

Similarly, the fatherstyle framework can be modified to fit the needs of the parent acting alone. We suggest a pragmatic approach. If what you're doing as a virtual single parent is working, stay the course. If it's not working, then consider adapting elements of fathersyle.

For example, if you are a woman with a husband who is so disengaged from the parenting process that it appears hopeless of any change, you may want to use some of the elements of fatherstyle, starting with play. You may be inclined to be reserved and mostly verbal in your play. But if you have an infant, toddler, or preschooler, instead of railing at your husband for never playing with your child, you just might start being more of a "Fatherstyle Mom." To do this, you can review both Chapters 2 and 5 and begin to be more physically engaging with your child. We think that when single (or virtually single) moms do a great job of raising a child, they have probably incorporated more than a little of the fatherstyle approach.

Composite Couples

As promised, we've created three composite couples, loosely based on real people we've known who face some common parenting challenges. We will discuss the differences in their parenting styles and their frustrations with continuing conflicts. We will then apply the fatherstyle framework to their specific situations and assess the effectiveness of the framework.

Couple 1: Susan and Mike

Susan and Mike have been married for eighteen years. They have four children ranging in age from seven to sixteen. Mike works long hours for a company that supplies parts for automobiles, and he travels frequently. Susan is an at-home mom who has recently returned to her previous career in accounting on a part-time basis. They live in a comfortable home in the newer suburbs.

Couple 2: Bill and Colleen

Bill and Colleen have been married for five years. They have four-year-old twin boys. They both work full time with flexible schedules: Bill runs his own contracting business and Colleen is a nurse, often on the late shift. They consider religion an important part of their lives and are considering having another child. They live in a modest home in an older suburb.

Couple 3: Kathleen and Tom

Kathleen and Tom have been married for ten years. They have three children, ages eight, six, and three, and they both work full-time. Kathleen is an ophthalmologist and Tom is a heart surgeon. They have a live-in nanny and a maid who handles the household chores. They live in a duplex co-op in a large city.

The Challenges

Susan and Mike consider their biggest challenge the lack of structure in their home. Because Mike's demanding job leaves him little time at home, the burden of child-rearing falls almost entirely on Susan's shoulders. She finds the job overwhelming, and as a result their family life is disorganized. Things are better now that all of the children are in school all day and Susan has some time away at her job, which she enjoys a great deal. But family meals are still rare, and Susan often feels that things are about to spin out of control.

Bill and Colleen's main issue is bedtime. Their boys share a bedroom and will not go to sleep until the whole family has endured an hours-long routine of screaming, crying, and general pandemonium. Even then, Colleen ends up pushing their beds together and sleeping with them a few nights a week. Another less pressing issue is the boys' continuing use of pacifiers and sippy cups throughout the day.

Kathleen and Tom's primary concern is their fundamental disagreement over their roles as parents. Tom thinks that his high-pressure career entitles him to free time spent away from the family. He golfs every weekend and even takes two short golfing trips with friends every year. Kathleen thinks that because they spend so much time at their jobs that their free time should be spent as a family. She resents having to juggle things while Tom is gone, and she secretly wishes she could spend time by herself, too.

The Fatherstyle Solutions

During several evening discussions over a two-month period, Susan and Mike assessed their situation. They agreed that their home life needed greater structure, but they differed on how to achieve it. Mike suggested that Susan quit her job and spend her free time during the day handling all of the household tasks so that she could focus on the children before and after school and on weekends. Susan protested that she would go over the edge without the challenge and diversion provided by her job and that Mike should take on more responsibility. After taking the quiz and discussing their motivations, Mike agreed to assess his role as a father. He also agreed to learn more about fatherstyle.

"I had to admit," Mike said, "I wasn't your typical father, although I thought I was. What I learned was that I was out of step with the times."

"He was bringing up his kids exactly the way he was brought up," Susan commented. "His idea of being a good father was to work hard, make lots of money, and turn over the day-to-day management of the household and the children to me."

As they talked about it, Mike had to admit that not only was he much like his own father, but that he missed out on great chunks of his children's lives. And he realized that he wished he had had a closer relationship with his own father.

"That's when I realized that the fathers I saw at the park when I drove by on those rare days when I was coming home when it was still light out were enjoying their roles as fathers," Mike said. "I felt bad that I wasn't doing more with my kids."

More important, as Mike and Susan continued to talk and learn more about the unique roles fathers play in raising kids, Mike realized that his children were missing out on important things that only he could provide. "I thought I was giving them all the advantages in life," Mike said sadly, "by providing a nice home, a good neighborhood, and expensive summer camps. But what they were missing out on was all the benefits of having an involved dad."

Susan and Mike finally came to a decision that pleased the whole family. Mike would cut back on work, spend more time with his family, and learn how to be the kind of father he wished he had when he was young.

Bill and Colleen were ready to go to a child psychologist when they decided to give the fatherstyle framework a chance. They took the parenting style quiz and they saw how different they were in their approaches to parenting. They also came to another realization: Bill usually gave in to Colleen's approach because, as he said, "She's the nurse and understands children."

Since he usually allowed her to handle bedtime as well as other discipline, Bill was relegated to a minor role as parent. In addition, he said he felt like "Colleen's assistant." "I tried to do things her way because she was better educated and I just believed she knew more about parenting," Bill said. But he began to appreciate that her approach wasn't working when it came to bedtime and other issues.

Although Colleen was defensive about admitting that her ways of dealing with the twins wasn't working, she was also frustrated by her own lack of success. She finally persuaded Bill that together they needed to learn more about fatherstyle. "And maybe, I remember saying to him," Colleen commented later, "his lack of training in child development or child psychology was a blessing. He could just do things the way he felt comfortable as a dad."

"When she said that," Bill said, "I felt liberated. It was like I didn't have to try to be Colleen junior as a parent."

As they both learned more about fatherstyle, Bill saw that what fathers often do when it comes to discipline and issues like bedtime, fit in with his own ideas about how things should be handled. "I'm in the construction business," Bill reasoned, "and what I know about is building houses. But I'm good at that and I'm really very organized and believe it or not the guys like working for me. So I must know something about human nature."

Bill convinced Colleen that he should try putting the boys to bed on his own for a couple of weeks. He didn't say it aloud to her, but he felt that she was babying the boys by giving in to their bedtime manipulation. Colleen agreed, even leaving the house for a few nights because the screaming was too much for her. Bill eventually got the boys into a settled routine of bath, stories, and bed.

"After two weeks, I was frankly amazed at what a good job Bill had done," Colleen admitted. But Bill said the same thing. "You know," he said, "my way worked pretty good. Our evenings are much quieter and Colleen and I actually get to spend more time together without the twins."

"Bill did such a good job with the bedtime problems," Colleen said, "I'm going to listen to his ideas more. Who knows, I may even let him handle the pacifier problem, too."

Kathleen and Tom are another story. After initially refusing to participate, Tom agreed to go through the motions of applying the fatherstyle framework. A lot of back and forth, including some yelling, convinced the couple that they were never going to agree. Tom liked being in control and dictating what others do. He said at first that his job was important and filled with unbelievable pressures. "I think I'm entitled to spending my free time as I wish," Tom declared.

"If you don't want to be married and have a family," Kathleen countered, "then we need to decide that now."

Tom said that her threats were unfair and that he liked being married and he wanted to enjoy his family. "You can't just enjoy your family on your terms," Kathleen said. "If you are going to be a husband and a father, you have to be as committed to that as you are to surgery and golf."

That struck home with Tom. "You're right," he said, "If I'm going to be a father, I should be the best father I can be."

But he admitted he really knew nothing about being a father. Kathleen suggested he attend a fathers group that his own hospital was putting on. Although he initially said that he didn't have time, Tom remembered his commitment and he reluctantly began attending the group.

"What I found were all these younger men," Tom said, "who wanted to enjoy their children and learn how to do it right. I guess after a few weeks of the group I got caught up in it, too."

One day, several months later, Tom told Kathleen that what he was learning in the fathers group had changed his attitudes and his thinking about his role as a dad. "My kids need me more than they need a nanny," he said. "You know, I'm beginning to see that being around my kids and playing with them can be as relaxing as golf. Probably a lot more relaxing, if you want to know the truth!"

Eventually, Kathleen and Tom worked out some compromises. Tom stopped scheduling some of the surgeries he used to take on. He agreed to coach a soccer team for his daughter. And he tried to make sure at least one day a weekend was devoted to his kids. "It's just me and them on either Saturday or Sunday, now," Tom said. "We just play or goof around and I'm getting a kick out it. I'm even thinking about taking them—just me and the kids—on a camping trip to Canada."

"He's come a long way," Kathleen said. "I can see a big difference in the kids and in him. Everybody is happier. And I think the heart surgeon actually is healthier because he's taking time to just play with his kids. He really ought to recommend that to all his patients!"

A Word About Single Parenting and Divorce

About fifty percent of first marriages end in divorce. That affects nearly a million children in the United States each year. This means that there are a great many co-parents living in different houses and trying to manage the difficult task of bringing up kids together.

Divorce can be the best answer to a loveless marriage or one that has become a constant battleground filled with endless arguments. Once a divorce has taken place, though, it is still up to both mom and dad to put aside their anger and arguments to come together at least sometimes to parent in the best interests of their children. It is our belief and experience that children can weather a split and even thrive after a divorce, as long as both parents stop any serious conflict and begin to handle their parenting responsibilities as mature adults.

In some instances, divorce leads to one or the other parent assuming a more involved role as parent. That can be a good thing. However, it still happens that when one co-parent claims "ownership" of the children and blocks a co-parenting and a fifty-fifty custody and parenting arrangement, then not only do the children suffer but it frequently happens that one parent (usually a father) bows out, leaving the other parent to carry on without his (or her) participation.

We would hope that if you are reading this book that you are committed to joint parenting and believe (as we do) that children need both parents in their lives because of the unique contribution of each parent. If this is so, then we trust that what you have learned from this book will inform your perceptions of your co-parent beginning to have a new (or renewed) respect for what he or she can bring to your child's development.

On the other hand, if you're divorced or have always been a single parent, you will understandably have a more difficult job ahead of you. However, by using the parenting techniques you've learned in this book, we think you will be a more highly skilled parent.

One of the long-standing critical comments of divorced mothers is that when the children are spending time with their dad they only play. This may well be the case, but the kind of play dads do is an important part of helping your children grow into socialized and successful young people. If you find, though, that between you and your co-parent you're both failing to provide the essential elements of fatherstyle, then this means it is time for reviewing the fatherstyle framework and seriously examining how together you will make sure your child receives all of the benefits of fatherstyle.

Go Team!

Being part of a team is rarely easy. We all want to do things our own way, and we naturally tend to blame our teammates for our errors. But there is no avoiding the reality that parenting is a team enterprise and that our children benefit the most if we approach it in that spirit. The whole message of this book is that *both* mothers and fathers have something unique and valuable to contribute to parenting and *that they can become better parents by learning from each other*. The challenge, of course, is to put aside ego and remember that we share the common goal of raising happy, healthy children who will have what it takes to become terrific parents themselves. Working together, we can do it.

Acknowledgments

No book ever gets written without plenty of help and support from many people. And while this project has been an enjoyable collaboration between friends, there are many other people who helped us in one way or another during the planning and writing of this book. Helping us with the initial task of clarifying our ideas were the skilled editor Beth Lieberman and our agent, Denise Marcil. We thank them both for their frank opinions and wise counsel. Beth helped us turn our swirl of ideas into a terrific proposal, contributing much to the ultimate shape and focus of the book as well. Denise deserves particular credit for understanding that we had something important to say and making sure we ended up saying it in the best possible way. Which, of course, led to us working with Stewart, Tabori & Chang and our editor, Jennifer Levesque, who was enthusiastic about this project from the beginning as well as a great champion of the book's message.

Furthermore, we owe a debt of gratitude to the many fathering experts we were able to meet and get to know over the years through our involvement with the Michigan Fathers Conference. It was through our annual conferences that we met Ross Parke, professor of psychology at the University of California–Riverside, and Kyle Pruett, clinical professor of child psychiatry and nursing at the Yale School of Medicine, who have served as intellectual and spiritual guides as we wrote this book. Ross Parke, in particular, was very willing to share his thoughts and his research with us during our writing. Jonathan Matanah, associate professor of psychology at Towson University in Maryland, was very helpful by helping locate research and commenting on the chapter on independence and autonomy.

Our families have been generous in letting us work on this book on Sunday afternoons, when we'd all have preferred doing something together. Extra special thanks to Molly and Jane.

And the book wouldn't have been possible without the helpfulness and willingness of many fathers to share their experiences. We would especially like to thank Bernard Gaulier, Dave Force, Adam Frost, Greg Austen, Rod Yeacker, Lori Hale, Katie Conti, Joanna Papiez, Paul Van Heulen, and Scott Allen, all of whom gave us helpful anecdotes and quotes that have enlivened this book. There were numerous other parents we talked to individually, in groups, or in a fathers panel, who were always kind enough to answer our many questions. Thanks to all of them.

Suggested Books and Web Resources for Parents

Books

Kyle Pruett. *Fatherneed: Why Father Care Is as Essential as Mother Care for Your Child.* New York: Broadway Books, 2000.

This groundbreaking book explains the latest research on the importance of involved fathering while challenging some of the things we think we know about mothers and fathers and how they relate to their children. This is an excellent resource for readers interested in finding out more about some of the research we cite throughout The Fatherstyle Advantage.

Ross D. Parke and Armin A. Brott. *Throwaway Dads: The Myths and Barriers That Keep Men from Becoming the Fathers They Want to Be.* New York: Houghton Mifflin, 1999.

In this book the authors explain how our culture's negative portrayal of dads "keeps fathers from being as actively involved as they'd like to be." This book debunks many persistent social images, from the over-hyped stereotype of the deadbeat dad to the myth of the dangerous male, and even offers advice on what dads can do to redefine their own roles in a positive way.

James A. Levine. *Working Fathers: New Strategies for Balancing Work and Family.* New York: Addison-Wesley, 1997.

This book is full of practical ideas and effective strategies to help fathers balance the demands of home and career. Much of his advice applies equally to working mothers. Dr. Levine offers suggestions that parents can incorporate immediately to enhance the quality of their work and family life.

Armin A. Brott. *The New Father series* (also available as a boxed set). *The Single Father: A Dad's Guide to Parenting Without a Partner.* New York: Abbeville Pres, 1999. *The Expectant Father: Facts, Tips, and Advice for Dads-To-Be.* New York: Abbeville Press, 2001. *The New Father: A Dad's Guide to the First Year.* New York: Abbeville Press, 2004.

These informative volumes are geared to fathers with children of different ages, from infancy on up. Brott writes in an easy style that sounds like your best friend who happens to be a naturally good dad. These books are full of practical, common-sense parenting advice that will help any father become more confident and involved. I think of them as the equivalent of the What to Expect... *books, but for dads.*

Lawrence J. Cohen. *Playful Parenting: A Bold New Way to Nurture Close Connections, Solve Behavior Problems, and Encourage Children's Confidence.* New York: Ballantine, 2002.

"Play is the essence of life." So quotes the author of this outstanding book. Though not written only for fathers, much of the discussion and advice about becoming a more playful parent will be of special interest to dads. Dr. Cohen talks about how fathers can use play, including roughhousing and wrestling, as a means to establish a lasting emotional connection with their children.

Mark O'Connell. *The Good Father: On Men, Masculinity, and Life in the Family.* New York: Scribner, 2005.

This book is most valuable for dads of older children. It explores the conflicts many men feel about the challenges of fatherhood. The author explains how men can help their families by embracing their own masculinity, using fascinating real-world case studies drawn from his experience as a private therapist.

Bruce Linton. Finding Time for Fatherhood: Men's Concerns as Parents. Berkeley: Berkeley Hills Books, 2000.

A no-nonsense guide to what fathers can do every day to become more involved in their children's lives. Shorter than some of the other recommended books, this is ideal for dads with little time because you don't have to read the entire book to get started right away.

Web Sites

www.thefatherstyleadvantage.com

This is our Web site, so we naturally place it first. It offers complete, updated information about this book as well as biographical profiles of the two of us, our parenting blogs, our appearance schedules, links to other excellent parenting sites, live web chats, and the opportunity to subscribe to our e-newsletter.

www.fatherhood.org

Site of the National Fatherhood Initiative, the nation's largest fatherhood education and advocacy organization. Terrific information on all sorts of topics of interest to dads, plus an online store and links to many other sites. This is the best all-around site for dads.

www.mrdad.com

Site of fatherhood author and expert Armin Brott. This site, designed with both mothers and fathers in mind, features advice and archived columns that address many of the issues that challenge parents the most. Brott includes some excellent advice for mothers about how they can help their fathers become more involved parents.

www.partnershipfordads.org

This is the Web site of Partnership for Dads, the nonprofit group founded by Kevin. Partnership for Dads works with existing institutions to help fathers become more involved parents. The site describes the group's programs and offers resources and links relevant to its mission.

www.fatherhoodproject.org

This is the site of James A. Levine's group. While it tends to be more academic, it contains excellent resources for working parents.

www.fathers.com

Created by the National Center for Fathering, fathers.com advertises itself as "the premier online resource for everyday dads." It offers research-based training, practical tips, and resources to help men be the involved fathers, grandfathers, and father figures their children need.

www.fathersforum.com

"The online resource for new and expectant fathers."

www.dadstoday.com

This site provides many articles of interest to parents.

www.interactivedadmagazine.com

This is an e-zine with unique information, product reviews, and essays of interest to fathers (and many mothers, too).

www.jameswindell.com

This Web site includes articles, columns, books, links, and much helpful information for parents.

www.rebeldad.com

This is an entertaining, opinionated, and often hilarious blog written by a stay-at-home dad. You don't have to be a full-time father to appreciate the humor, however; it's always good for a big laugh. It gets a strong recommendation.

Selected Sources

Chapter 1

Barnett, Rosalind, and Caryl Rivers. *Same Difference: How Gender Myths Are Hurting Our Relationships, Our Children, and Our Jobs.* New York: Basic Books, 2004.

Belluck, Pam. "With Mayhem at Home, They Call a Parent Coach." *New York Times,* March 13, 2005.

Douglas, Susan J., and Meredith W. Michaels. *The Mommy Myth: The Idealization of Motherhood and How It Has Undermined Women.* New York: Free Press, 2004.

Gill, Libby. *Stay-at-Home Dads: The Essential Guide to Creating the New Family.* New York: Plume, 2001.

Lamb, Michael J. *The Role of the Father in Child Development.* New York: John Wiley & Sons, 1976.

Levine, J. A., and Todd L. Pittinsky. *Working Fathers: New Strategies for Balancing Work and Family.* New York: Addison-Wesley, 1997.

Parke, Ross D., and Armin A. Brott. *Throwaway Dads: The Myths and Barriers That Keep Men from Becoming the Fathers They Want to Be.* New York: Houghton Mifflin, 1999.

Pruett, Kyle. *Fatherneed: Why Father Care Is as Essential as Mother Care for Your Child.* New York: Broadway Books, 2000.

Tannen, Deborah. *You Just Don't Understand: Women and Men in Conversation.* New York: William Morrow & Co, 1990.

Waldman, Ayelet. "My Husband, The Perfect Mom." *Parenting* (November 2004): 81.

Chapter 2

Akers, M., and G. Lewis. *Good Sports: Athletes Your Kids Can Look Up To.* Dallas: Beckett Publications, 2001.

Biringen, Zeynep. *Raising a Secure Child: Creating an Emotional Connection Between You and Your Child.* New York: Perigee, 2004.

Borba, Michele. *Building Moral Intelligence.* San Francisco, CA: Jossey-Bass, 2001.

Cohen, Lawrence J. *Playful Parenting: A Bold New Way to Nurture Close Connections, Solve Behavior Problems, and Encourage Children's Confidence.* New York: Ballantine, 2002.

Franzini, Louis. *Kids Who Laugh: How To Develop Your Child's Sense of Humor.* Garden City, NY: Square One Publications, 2002.

Gill, Libby. *Stay-at-Home Dads: The Essential Guide to Creating the New Family.* New York: Plume, 2001.

Hoyt, Carolyn. "Making the Most of Dad Time." *Parenting* (January 2005): 138.

Leong, D. J., and E. Bodrova. "Playing to Learn." *Scholastic Parent and Child* (October 2003): 28.

Lieberman, Alicia F. *The Emotional Life of the Toddler.* New York: Free Press, 1993.

Parke, Ross D., and Armin A. Brott. *Throwaway Dads: The Myths and Barriers That Keep Men from Becoming the Fathers They Want to Be.* New York: Houghton Mifflin, 1999.

Pollack, William. *Real Boys: Rescuing Our Sons from the Myths of Boyhood.* New York: Henry Holt, 1998.

Popenoe, David. *Life Without Father: Compelling New Evidence That Fatherhood and Marriage Are Indispensable for the Good of Children and Society.* Cambridge: Harvard University Press, 1999.

Pruett, Kyle. *Fatherneed: Why Father Care Is as Essential as Mother Care for Your Child.* New York: Broadway Books, 2000.

Sears, W., and M. Sears. *The Successful Child: What Parents Can Do to Help Children Turn Out Well.* New York: Little Brown, 2002.

Chapter 3

Biller, Henry. *Fathers and Families.* Westport, CT: Auburn House/Greenwood Publishing Group, Inc., 1993.

Erikson, Erik. *Childhood and Society*. New York: Norton, 1963.

Grolnick, W. S., and R. M. Ryan. "Parent Styles Associated with Children's Self-Regulation and Competence in School." *Journal of Educational Psychology* 81, no. 2 (1989): 143–54.

Grolnick, W. S., and M. L. Slowiaczek. "Parents' Involvement in Children's Schooling: A Multidimensional Conceptualization and Motivational Model." *Child Development* 65 (1994): 237–52.

Grossman, F. K., W. S. Pollack, and E. Golding. "Fathers and Children: Predicting the Quality and Quantity of Fathering." *Developmental Psychology* 24, no. 1 (1988): 82–91.

Mattanah, Jonathan F. "Parental Psychological Autonomy and Children's Academic Competence and Behavioral Adjustment in Late Childhood: More Than Just Limit-Setting and Warmth." *Merrill-Palmer Quarterly* 47, no. 3 (2001): 355–76.

Morrongiello, B. A., and K. Hogg. "Mothers' Reactions to Children Misbehaving in Ways that Can Lead to Injury: Implications for Gender Differences in Children's Risk Taking and Injuries." *Sex Roles: A Journal of Research* 50, no. 1/2 (2004): 1103–18.

Morrongiello, B. A., and K. Hogg. "Toddlers' and Mothers' Behaviors in an Injury-Risk Situation: Implications for Sex Differences in Childhood Injuries." *Journal of Applied Developmental Psychology* 19, no. 4 (1998): 625–39.

Power, T. G., and J. Shanks. "Parents as Socializers: Maternal and Paternal Views." *Journal of Youth and Adolescence* 18 (1989): 203–20.

Pruett, Kyle. *Fatherneed: Why Father Care Is as Essential as Mother Care for Your Child.* New York: Broadway Books, 2000.

Chapter 4

Gilligan, Carol. *In a Different Voice: Psychological Theory and Women's Development.* Cambridge: Harvard University Press, 1982.

LeFebvre, Joan E. "Fathers are Important." *Parenting the Preschooler* (May 2003). www.uwex.edu/ces/flp/pp/

Power, T. G., M. P. McGrath, S. O. Hughes, and S. H. Manire. "Compliance and Self-assertion: Young Children's Responses to Mothers versus Fathers." *Developmental Psychology* 30, no. 6 (1994): 980–89.

Pruett, Kyle. *Fatherneed: Why Father Care is as Essential as Mother Care for Your Child.* New York: Broadway Books, 2000.

Tannen, Deborah. *I Only Say This Because I Love You.* New York: Ballantine Books, 2002.

Tannen, Deborah. *That's Not What I Meant.* New York: Ballantine Books, 1987.

Chapter 5

Bernadette-Shapiro, S., D. Ehrensaft, and J. L. Shapiro. "Father Participation in Childcare and the Development of Empathy in Sons: An Empirical Study." *Family Therapy* 23, no. 2 (1996): 77–93.

Goleman, Daniel. *Emotional Intelligence.* New York: Bantam Books, 1995.

Koestner, F., and J. Weinberger. "The Family Origins of Empathic Concerns: A 26-Year Longitudinal Study." *Journal of Personality and Social Psychology* 58 (1990): 709–17.

Radke-Yarrow, M., and C. Zahn-Waxler. "Roots, Motives and Patterns in Children's Prosocial Behavior," in *Development and Maintenance of Prosocial Behavior*, edited by Ervin Stabu et al. New York: Plenum, 1984.

Sears, R. R., E. E. Maccoby, and H. Levin. *Patterns of Child Rearing.* Evanston, IL: Row, Peterson & Co., 1957.

Shapiro, Lawrence E. *How to Raise a Child with a High EQ: A Parents' Guide to Emotional Intelligence.* New York: HarperPerennial, 1998.

Chapter 6

Barber, J., N. Parizeau, and N. Bergman. *Spark Your Child's Success in Math and Science.* Berkeley, CA: Great Explorations, 2002.

Fuller, Cheri. *Raising Motivated Kids.* Bedford, OH: Pinon Press, 2004.

Gilbert, Susan. *A Field Guide to Boys and Girls.* New York: Harper Perennial, 2001.

McCaffrey, B. R. National Youth Anti-Drug Media Campaign Press Release. "White House Drug Czar Underscores Dads' Important Role in Keeping Kids Drug Free." Washington, D.C., Office of National Drug Control Policy, June 12, 2000.

Pruett, Kyle. *Fatherneed: Why Father Care is as Essential as Mother Care for Your Child.* New York: Broadway Books, 2000.

Ryan, K., and K. E. Bohlin. *Building Character in Schools.* San Francisco, CA: Jossey-Bass, 1999.

Sears, W., and M. Sears. *The Successful Child: What Parents Can Do to Help Children Turn Out Well.* New York: Little Brown, 2002.

Taylor, Jim. *Positive Pushing: How to Raise a Successful and Happy Child.* New York: Hyperion, 2002.

Witmer, Denise D. *The Everything Parent's Guide to Raising a Successful Child.* New York: Avon, 2004.

Chapter 7

Fisher, R., B. M. Patton, and W. L. Ury. *Getting to Yes: Negotiating Agreement without Giving In.* (2nd ed.) New York: Houghton Mifflin, 1992.

Tannen, Deborah. *I Only Say This Because I Love You: How the Way We Talk Can Make or Break Family Relationships Throughout Our Lives.* New York: Random House, 2001.

Tannen, Deborah. *You Just Don't Understand: Women and Men in Conversation.* New York: William Morrow & Co, 1990.

Index

Q

R